WPS News
September 2024

Copyright Cliff Potts 2024

Forward

The Ethical Dilemma of Doing Business in China: A Complex Tapestry

Doing business in China presents a unique set of ethical challenges that companies must navigate. Here are some key dilemmas:

Human Rights Concerns

- **Forced Labor:** Allegations of forced labor, particularly in Xinjiang, where Uyghur Muslims are detained in re-education camps, raise concerns about supply chain ethics.
- **Worker Rights:** Ensuring fair wages, safe working conditions, and freedom of association can be difficult in a country with a history of labor abuses.

Intellectual Property Rights

- **Piracy:** China has a reputation for intellectual property theft, making it challenging for companies to protect their innovations and brand reputation.
- **Forced Technology Transfer:** Companies may be pressured to share proprietary technology with Chinese partners as a condition of doing business.

Censorship and Surveillance

- **Internet Restrictions:** The Great Firewall of China limits access to information and online platforms, raising concerns about freedom of expression and privacy.
- **Surveillance State:** China's extensive surveillance network, including facial recognition and social credit systems, raises ethical questions about data privacy and individual liberties.

Environmental Impact

- **Pollution:** China's rapid industrialization has led to significant environmental degradation, including air and water pollution.
- **Resource Depletion:** The country's demand for natural resources, such as rare earth minerals, can contribute to global environmental issues.

Corporate Social Responsibility

- **Balancing Profits and Ethics:** Companies must weigh the potential for profit against the ethical implications of their operations in China.
- **Engaging with the Chinese Government:** Navigating the complex political landscape and engaging with government officials can present ethical challenges.

Case Study: Apple and Human Rights

Apple, a major player in the global tech industry, has faced criticism for its reliance on Chinese suppliers. Reports of poor working conditions, including long hours and low wages, have raised questions about the company's commitment to ethical sourcing.

Addressing the Dilemma

To navigate these ethical challenges, companies can consider the following strategies:

- **Due Diligence:** Conduct thorough audits of suppliers to ensure compliance with labor and environmental standards.
- **Transparency:** Disclose supply chain information and publicly report on social and environmental impact.
- **Engagement:** Work with suppliers and the Chinese government to promote ethical practices.
- **Risk Assessment:** Identify potential risks and develop mitigation strategies.
- **Ethical Leadership:** Foster a strong ethical culture within the company and hold employees accountable for ethical behavior.

Doing business in China is a complex endeavor. By understanding and addressing these ethical dilemmas, companies can balance economic interests with social and environmental responsibility.

September Serenade: Unveiling the Philippines' Untamed Beauty

Welcome September

September in the Philippines strikes a captivating chord. It's a month of contrasts, where the remnants of the rainy season dance with the promise of drier days. Lush landscapes glisten with rainwater, and the air hums with a quiet anticipation. This unique period unveils the Philippines in a light unlike any other, offering a glimpse into its breathtaking natural beauty, interwoven with the deep-rooted Catholic traditions and the ever-present love for the Christmas season.

While the downpours may linger, September paints the Philippines with a vibrant emerald palette. Rice paddies shimmer, their verdant hues reflecting the playful dance of sunlight breaking through the clouds. Waterfalls, awakened from their rainy season slumber, cascade down verdant slopes, creating a symphony of sound and movement. This verdant tapestry is a paradise for nature enthusiasts. Imagine trekking through the misty jungles of Batanes, or exploring the hidden coves of Coron, their lush beauty amplified by the recent rains.

However, the beauty of September in the Philippines extends beyond its landscapes. This month marks the unofficial beginning of the "ber months," the Filipino countdown to Christmas. While it may seem unusual, this period reflects the deep Catholic faith embedded in Filipino culture. Churches come alive with anticipation as communities begin preparing for the festive season. September serenades are a common sight, with families and friends gathering outside churches, singing hymns that herald the approaching Christmas spirit. This unique tradition paints a heartwarming picture of a nation where faith and family intertwine.

The love for Christmas in September isn't limited to religious practices. Decorations begin to appear in malls and public spaces, a gentle reminder of the impending joyous season. The spirit of generosity flourishes, with communities organizing charity drives and preparing for gift-giving traditions. This period offers a glimpse into the heart of the Filipino people, a nation where celebration and compassion go hand in hand.

September in the Philippines is a month of both serenity and anticipation. It's a time to witness the untamed beauty of a nation, its landscapes pulsating with the lifeblood of the recent rains. It's a month to experience the deep-rooted Catholic traditions and the infectious love for the Christmas season, a cultural phenomenon unlike any other. September in the Philippines is a vibrant serenade, an invitation to experience a country where nature's beauty and cultural richness create a truly unforgettable experience.

Discover more from WPS News

Subscribe to get the latest posts sent to your email.

Letter Seven: Empowering Voices Through Virtual Town Halls: Ensuring Inclusivity and Engagement

In today's fast-paced world, it is more important than ever to ensure that every voice is heard, especially when it comes to community matters. With the rise of technology and virtual communication tools, we have a powerful opportunity to bridge the gap and create spaces for meaningful dialogue and participation. One such tool that has gained prominence, especially in the wake of the COVID-19 pandemic, is the virtual town hall meeting conducted through platforms like Zoom.

Harnessing Technology for Community Engagement

Virtual town halls represent a powerful avenue for community engagement, allowing individuals to come together, share their thoughts, and actively participate in discussions about what is happening in their community. However, to truly harness the potential of these virtual gatherings and prevent anyone from being silenced by the system, it is crucial to implement certain key strategies.

Promoting Inclusivity and Participation

First and foremost, promoting inclusivity is paramount. It is essential to ensure that all community members are aware of these virtual town halls and are encouraged to participate. Using a variety of communication channels and outreach methods can help reach a diverse audience and make sure that everyone feels welcome to share their perspectives.

Providing Multiple Pathways for Expression

Providing multiple ways to participate is another critical aspect. Not everyone may feel comfortable speaking up in a large virtual meeting, so offering options for submitting questions or comments anonymously, or through written submissions, can help ensure that all voices are heard, regardless of their preferred mode of communication.

Establishing Guidelines for Constructive Dialogue

Establishing ground rules for respectful communication during the town hall is also essential. By setting guidelines and expectations for behavior, participants can feel assured that their contributions will be valued and that discussions will remain constructive and focused on the issues at hand.

The Role of Skilled Moderation in Facilitating Discussions

Effective moderation is key to ensuring that the virtual town hall runs smoothly and that everyone gets a chance to speak. Skilled moderators can manage the flow of the meeting, facilitate discussions, and ensure that diverse perspectives are represented and respected.

Recording Sessions for Accessibility and Reference

Recording and sharing the sessions can further enhance inclusivity. By making the town hall recordings available for those who couldn't attend live, the conversation can reach a wider audience and serve as a valuable resource for future discussions and decision-making processes.

Gathering Feedback for Continuous Improvement

Finally, collecting feedback from participants after each town hall is crucial for continuous improvement. By listening to the community's input and suggestions, organizers can refine their approach and make sure that future virtual town halls are even more effective in giving everyone a voice.

Building a Platform for All Voices to Be Heard

In conclusion, virtual town halls represent a powerful tool for empowering voices and fostering community engagement. By promoting inclusivity, providing multiple participation options, setting ground rules, effective moderation, recording sessions, and collecting feedback, we can create a space where everyone feels heard, valued, and empowered to shape the future of their community. Let us embrace the opportunities that technology offers and continue to use it to our benefit in ensuring that no voice goes unheard in the conversations that matter most.

Cliff Potts

Discover more from WPS News
Subscribe to get the latest posts sent to your email.

A Comparative Analysis: The American Civil War and WWII in Europe

The American Civil War (1861-1865) and World War II in Europe (1939-1945) were two major conflicts that shaped the course of history in profound ways. Both wars involved deep-seated racial ideologies that influenced the actions of the belligerents – the Confederates in the Civil War and the Nazis in WWII. Furthermore, the aftermath of these conflicts saw the United States grappling with the legacies of traitors and war criminals in different ways.

Racist Theosophy of the Confederates and Nazis

The Confederates in the American Civil War and the Nazis in World War II shared a common thread of racist ideology that sought to justify their actions through a warped sense of racial superiority. The Confederates believed in the institution of slavery as essential to their way of life, viewing African Americans as inferior and deserving of subjugation. This belief was enshrined in their secession documents and was a central tenet of their cause.

Similarly, the Nazis under Adolf Hitler espoused a racist doctrine that culminated in the Holocaust, the systematic genocide of six million Jews and millions of others deemed undesirable by the regime. The Nazis believed in the concept of a "master race" and sought to eradicate those they deemed racially inferior, such as Jews, Romani people, and disabled individuals.

Comparing the Wars

The American Civil War and WWII in Europe differed in scope, scale, and global impact. The Civil War was a domestic conflict fought primarily over the issue of slavery and the secession of Southern states from the Union. It resulted in over 600,000 deaths and the abolition of slavery in the United States.

In contrast, WWII was a global conflict involving multiple countries and theaters of war. It resulted in the deaths of over 70 million people and the devastation of much of Europe. The war ended with the defeat of the Axis powers, including Nazi Germany, and the establishment of the United Nations to prevent future conflicts.

Dealing with Traitors and War Criminals

After the American Civil War, the United States faced the challenge of reconstructing the Southern states and reintegrating former Confederates into the Union. While Confederate leaders were granted amnesty and pardons by President Andrew Johnson, the process of Reconstruction was marred by continued racial violence and discrimination against African Americans.

In contrast, after WWII, the Allies held the Nuremberg Trials to prosecute prominent Nazi leaders for war crimes and crimes against humanity. The trials established the principle of individual accountability for atrocities committed during wartime and set a precedent for future international criminal tribunals.

Cultural Legacy of the Civil War in the USA

As of 2020, the United States continues to grapple with the cultural legacy of the Civil War, particularly regarding issues of race, identity, and historical memory. Debates over the display of Confederate symbols, the renaming of military bases named after Confederate generals, and the teaching of Civil War history in schools reflect the ongoing struggle to confront the nation's past and its implications for the present.

In conclusion, the American Civil War and WWII in Europe were defining moments in history that shaped the course of nations and societies. Both conflicts were marked by racist ideologies that influenced the actions of the belligerents and left a lasting impact on subsequent generations. The ways in which the US dealt with traitors and war criminals in the aftermath of these conflicts reflect the complex and contested nature of historical memory and national identity.

Discover more from WPS News
Subscribe to get the latest posts sent to your email.

Be Future-Savvy: Decoding South China Sea Tensions 2025-2035 | WPS.News

Yo Millennials & Zoomers: South China Sea Drama Ain't Going Anywhere – WPS.News Got You Prepped (2025-2035)

Alright, fam, let's talk real. Scrolling through endless memes is fun, but the world's got some serious issues brewing, and one that's gonna keep popping up: the South China Sea tensions. We know, geopolitics sounds like a snoozefest, but hear us out, Zoomers and Millennials. This ain't just some faraway land dispute, it's gonna impact EVERYTHING from trade routes to your favorite gadgets in the next decade (2025-2035). Buckle up, because WPS.News is here to decode the drama and make you future-savvy on the Indo-Pacific.

Why Should You Care About the South China Sea?

Yeah, yeah, you might be thinking, "Why should I care about some random sea in Asia?" Here's the lowdown:

- **It's a Trade Hotspot:** Imagine your online shopping addiction on steroids. The South China Sea is a vital shipping lane for trillions of dollars worth of goods every year. If things get messy, those deliveries could get disrupted, impacting everything from your phone's price to the cost of that next-day delivery.
- **Energy Bonanza (But Also Conflict Zone):** The South China Sea is sitting on a treasure trove of oil and gas reserves. Big players like China and Vietnam are scrambling to claim these resources, and tensions can easily escalate. Think of it as a real-life game of Risk, but with way higher stakes.
- **Military Muscle Flexing:** This ain't just an economic tug-of-war. China's been building artificial islands and flexing its military muscle in the region. Other countries, like the US, are sending warships to counter this, raising the risk of a major conflict.

Basically, the South China Sea is a simmering pot of geopolitical drama that could boil over and impact the entire world, including you (and your online shopping habits).

WPS.News: Your Guide to the Indo-Pacific Future (2025-2035)

So, what can WPS.News do for you? We're not just gonna bombard you with boring political jargon. We'll break down the complex issues like:

- **China's Rise as a Superpower:** China's influence is growing, and the South China Sea is a key part of its strategy. We'll analyze China's economic and military ambitions and what they mean for the future of the region. This ain't just about history class anymore, fam. Knowing China's plans can help you make informed decisions about your future careers and travel destinations.
- **The US Indo-Pacific Pivot:** The US ain't letting China have all the fun. We'll explain how the US is shifting its focus towards the Indo-Pacific region to counter China's influence. Understanding this 'pivot' is crucial, as it will shape alliances and military deployments, impacting everything from global security to travel restrictions.
- **The Rise of Regional Players:** Don't underestimate the smaller countries in the region! Vietnam, Indonesia, and the Philippines all have a stake in the South China Sea. We'll keep you updated on how these countries are asserting themselves on the world stage. Knowing these rising stars could be a major advantage if you're thinking of studying abroad or working in the region.
- **The Power of Diplomacy (and Maybe a Little Tech):** We might not have flying cars yet, but technology will play a big role in the South China Sea dispute. We'll explore how drones, advanced radars, and even artificial intelligence are shaping how countries monitor and manage the region. Understanding these technological advancements could open doors to future career opportunities in these fields.

But wait, there's more! Here's how reading WPS.News can actually benefit you:

- **Be a Global Citizen:** Knowing what's going on in the world makes you a more informed and responsible citizen.
- **Travel Smarter:** The South China Sea tensions could impact travel restrictions and safety in the region. We'll keep you updated on potential hotspots, so you can plan your dream vacation with confidence.
- **Career Advantage:** Understanding the Indo-Pacific will be a major asset in a globalized job market. Companies are looking for employees with a strong grasp of international affairs.
- **Invest Wisely:** Geopolitical tensions can impact the stock market. Reading WPS.News can help you make informed investment decisions based on real-world trends.

The Future Ain't Written, But You Can Be Ready for It: WPS.News is your compass through the complex world of the South China Sea tensions. Stay informed, stay ahead, and make the next decade your own.

Discover more from WPS News
Subscribe to get the latest posts sent to your email.

Respecting Filipino Hospitality: An Expat's Reflection

Today is my 1st anniversary in the Philippines. My wife, and my son grew up here. This is their country. I call this archipelago home now, yet I am a guest, and I know it. I am still working on becoming conversational in Tagalog, and Bisdak (A.K.A. Cebuano or Visayan). That is not an easy task. I am still trying to navigate the politics and the cultural references. These are wonderful people. They absolutely do live up to their reputation of being hospitable. If you get an opportunity to take a world class vacation, add the Philippines to your destination.

The one thing I do try to stay clear of here is the internal politics of the nation. It is nor a matter of not understanding the politics here. I have read enough to have a clue of the general issues of this nation of 116 Million souls. Though, as I have said, "I am a guest here." I am only concerned with the issues which negatively impact my little family, and her extended family. For that reason I am vigilant on the issues about the encroachment of China in the Exclusive Economic Zones of the Philippines and, on occasion, Filipino territorial waters. The Chinese do nor belong here.

Without having a surface vessel, or the seafaring skills of the local fisherfolk, all I can do right now is write about it and keep people informed about what is going on. I am working on changing my skill set to gain more nautical abilities, however, that is still a ways off.

In the meantime, I will keep working on what I can, and living my life with the people who do love me here. I am grateful that I found this life, and my love,

Discover more from WPS News
Subscribe to get the latest posts sent to your email.

Religious Influence in Politics: Historical Lessons for the Future

One of the internet's many hit-and-run-artists decided to ask a question on one of my web logs a few months ago. The question was "Why do you think you have all the answers?"

The question is nonsense, plain and simple. The internet is filled with people who use the anonymity of the web to be excessively rude and argumentative. If the person had bothered to read anything I had posted, she would have figured out that I don't think I have all the answers. I am, like many, groping in the descending darkness, trying to define a line of tactical response to the events of our day. I am not trying to exalt or glorify myself as being some kind of cosmically defined leader. I am but one soul who, with the aid of history, sees a nation descending into troubled times. What history, you may ask? Read the words of Adolph Hitler below:[1]

The national government will maintain and defend the foundations on which the power of our nation rests. It will offer strong protection to Christianity as the very basis of our collective morality.

Today Christians stand at the head of our country. We want to fill our culture again with the Christian spirit. We want to burn out all the recent immoral developments in literature, in the theater, and in the press — in short, we want to burn out the poison of immorality which has entered into our whole life and culture as a result of LIBERAL excess during the past years.[2]

I believe today that I am acting in the sense of the Almighty Creator… I am fighting for the Lord's Work.[3]

The [National Government] regards Christianity as the foundation of our national morality, and the family as the basis of national life.[4]

***

Secular schools can never be tolerated because such a school has no religious instruction and a general moral instruction without a religious foundation is built on air; consequently, all character training and religion must be derived from faith…. We need believing people.[5]

I hope to live to see the day when, as in the early days of our country, we won't give any public schools. The churches will have taken over again and Christians will be running them. What a happy day that will be![6]

The first quote above is from Adolph Hitler; the second quote is from Jerry Falwell. Not only do Falwell's words almost exactly match what Hitler said in 1933, but also his beliefs are the foundation of a theocratic state. Manifest Destiny came out of such theocratic institutions. Ask Native Americans how they feel about such teachings. There is more evidence of the disdain with which the neo-conservative community holds the rule of law in the United States.

The Supreme Court of the Unites States of America is an institution damned by God Almighty.[7]

That statement matches much of the rhetoric in the pre-Civil War days of the late 1850s.

I believe this notion of the separation of Church and State was the figment of some infidel's imagination.[8]

It is interesting to note the past tense used in the statement and the date; the statement was made well over 20 years ago.

The majority of our leaders are pro-abortion. Therefore, you don't say, "I'm an advocate against abortion." No, you say:

I'm interested in housing, or development, or sanitation. And you keep your personal views to yourself until the Christian community is ready to rise up, and then, Wow! They're going to be devastated![9]

I want to be invisible. I do guerrilla warfare. I paint my face and travel at night. You don't know it's over until you're in a body bag.[10]

In January of 1994, Vice-President Dan Quayle spoke at a training conference of religious-right activists in Fort Lauderdale. The conference's theme was Reclaiming America, and before the event began Quayle stood at attention as the crowd of more than two thousand rose, faced the flag with a cross on it, and with hands on hearts, recited in unison, "I pledge allegiance to the Christian flag, and to our savior, crucified, risen, and coming again, with life and liberty for all who believe."[11]

The idea that religion and politics don't mix was invented by the Devil to keep Christians from running their own country.[12]

When I said during my presidential bid that I would only bring Christians and Jews into the government, I hit a firestorm. 'What do you mean?' the media challenged me. 'You're not going to bring atheists into the government? How dare you maintain that those who believe in the Judeo-Christian values are better qualified to govern America than Hindus and Muslims?' My simple answer is, `Yes, they are.[13]

The Spanish Inquisition, first imposed in Spain in 1478 and expanded by Holy Roman Emperor Charles V to the Netherlands in 1521, promoted the questioning and burning of "heretics" under government auspices. Speaking as a heretic (a Gnostic), I would not take kindly to be questioned or burned due to my particular belief system.

With the apathy that exists today, a small, well-organized minority can influence the selection of candidates to an astonishing degree.[14]

This Republican Party of Lincoln has become a party of theocracy.[15]

It is accepted that we do ignore the lessons of History. George Santayana said, "Those who cannot learn from history are doomed to repeat it."

George Wilhelm Hegel said, "What experience and history teach is this – that people and governments never have learned anything from history, or acted on principles."

George Bernard Shaw believed, "We learn from history that we learn nothing from history."

All of this points to a cataclysmic confrontation with destiny that has not been seen since World War II.

Do I have any answers, let alone all the answers? I have one answer. We do not have to repeat past mistakes; if we choose to talk, listen, and learn from one another and from our collective past we can avert the judgment of history. Barring that, we will once again go down the road of chaos and horror. At some point in the future, the sun of reason, intelligence, and wisdom will break through the clouds of darkness, fear, hate, cynicism, and judgment.

It is up to you to define the answers of our collective future. Even our friend, who did not take the time to find out the answer to her question, has the future in her hands…if she has the intelligence to manifest it in wisdom for the good of all.

[1] I can no longer recall the source of all the quotes from Hitler. In due diligence, I have searched for the source of the quotes to no avail.

[2] Adolph Hitler; Taken from The Speeches of Adolph Hitler, 1922-1939, Vol. 1, Michael Hakeem, Ph.D. (London, Oxford University Press, 1942), pp. 871-872. The Book Your Church Doesn't …, Leedom, p.265

[3] Adolph Hitler in 1938, The Book Your Church Doesn't …, Leedom, p. 292

[4] Hitler

[5] Adolf Hitler, April 26, 1933

[6] Rev. Jerry Falwell, 1979

[7] Rev. Jimmy Swaggart, 1986

[8] Rev. W.A. Criswell, Dallas, TX

, 1984

[9] Antonio Rivera, Christian Coalition, NYC, 1992

[10] Ralph Reed, Christian Coalition, 1991

[11] Sidney Blumenthal, New Yorker, July 18, 1994

[12] Rev. Jerry Falwell

[13] Pat Robertson, The New World Order, page 218

[14] Pat Robertson, The Millennium, 1990

[15] U.S. Representative Christopher Shays, R-CT. I would suggest that you visit the site Theocracy Watch

(http://www.theocracywatch.org/) for more information on the threat posed by the Neo-Conservative Right

Kevin Phillips in his recently published American Theocracy, states, "We can begin by describing the role of religion in American Politics with two words: Widely underestimated." Religion and politics are incredibly intertwined in the U.S., as they were in Europe before the foundation of the U.S.; and, that influence has been overlooked by the Establishment. Yet, George Gallop, the famous pollster, said, "religious affiliation remains one of the most accurate and least-appreciated political indicators available." (Potts, Clifford A. Radicals, Religion, and Revelation. 1st ed. Dallas: WordTechs Press, 2008. 5-6. CD-ROM).

Discover more from WPS News

Subscribe to get the latest posts sent to your email.

Letter Eight: Navigating the Era of Misinformation and Polarization: Building Unity in a Divided World

In today's interconnected world, the rise of misinformation, polarization, and distrust has cast a shadow over society, creating fractures in relationships and institutions. These challenges are not new but have been exacerbated in recent years, leading to a deepening sense of division and discord among people. As we reflect on the current state of affairs, it becomes evident that addressing these issues requires a collective effort to foster understanding, empathy, and unity.

The Seeds of Discord: A Look Back at History

The roots of our current societal challenges can be traced back to pivotal moments in history, such as the contentious 2000 election in the United States. The decision by the Supreme Court in favor of the Republicans in Florida set a precedent that raised questions about the integrity of democratic processes and fueled suspicions of manipulation and power plays. This event marked a turning point, where the lines between accepted norms and individual interests became blurred, setting the stage for the erosion of trust and the proliferation of misinformation.

From Politics to Personal: The Ripple Effects of Division

The impact of political discord and misinformation extends beyond the realm of governance, seeping into personal relationships and everyday interactions. The strain theory, which posits that societal goals and means are no longer shared or accepted, has become increasingly relevant in a world where diverging perspectives and conflicting narratives shape our interactions. This erosion of common ground has led to heightened tensions, creating a breeding ground for social upheaval and discord.

A Call for Unity: Navigating the Current Landscape

As we navigate these turbulent times, it is crucial to resist the temptation to retreat into isolation or resignation. Building bridges of understanding, empathy, and respect is essential for overcoming polarization and misinformation. By engaging in open dialogue, seeking out diverse perspectives, and promoting critical thinking, we can work towards a more inclusive and cohesive society.

Towards a Brighter Future: Embracing Collective Action

While the challenges we face may seem daunting, there is hope in our collective ability to effect positive change. By actively participating in efforts to combat misinformation, promote unity, and foster dialogue, we can contribute to a more harmonious and understanding world. It is through our shared commitment to empathy, respect, and cooperation that we can build a future where division gives way to unity, and discord transforms into harmony.

In conclusion, as we stand at a crossroads in history, it is imperative that we confront the issues of misinformation and polarization head-on, with a steadfast commitment to building bridges and fostering understanding. By embracing unity as a guiding principle, we can navigate the complexities of our times and strive towards a brighter future for all.

Cliff Potts

No Easy Catch:
The Struggle of Fisherfolk Against Industrial Fishing

The ocean provides life and livelihoods for millions of people worldwide, but for many fisherfolk, the future looks bleak. Large-scale industrial fishing, particularly by fleets like China's distant-water fishing fleet (DWF), is putting immense pressure on fish stocks and coastal communities.

Here's why small-scale fisherfolk are struggling:

- Resource Depletion: Massive fishing vessels can catch huge amounts of fish, leaving less for smaller, traditional fishing operations. This can lead to declining fish populations and smaller catches for fisherfolk.
- Illegal Fishing Practices: Some DWF vessels are accused of using illegal gear or fishing in restricted areas, further harming fish stocks and harming the environment.
- Unfair Competition: Large-scale fishing operations often benefit from government subsidies, making it harder for small-scale fishers to compete.
- Livelihoods at Risk: With fewer fish and unfair competition, fisherfolk struggle to make a living. This can impact their families and communities who depend on fishing for food and income.

A glimmer of hope: *The Stealth Runner*

While the challenges are significant, there are potential solutions on the horizon. Technologies like My Stealth Runner offer a promising approach. This can help:

- Combat Illegal Fishing: By monitoring vessel locations and activities, My Stealth Runner can deter illegal fishing practices and expose offenders.
- Protect Marine Resources: By providing data on fishing activity, My Stealth Runner can inform better management of fish stocks and promote sustainable fishing practices.
- Empower Fisherfolk: Access to this technology can empower fisherfolk to protect their fishing grounds and advocate for their rights.

What Can We Do?

There are ways to support sustainable fishing practices and protect the livelihoods of fisherfolk:

- **Buy Local Seafood:** Seek out fish caught by local, sustainable fisheries.

- **Demand Transparency:** Support organizations that promote responsible fishing practices and expose illegal activities.
- **Advocate for Change:** Urge governments to implement stricter regulations on industrial fishing and support policies that promote sustainable fishing practices.
- **Support The Stealth Runner:** Look for ways to advocate for or contribute to the development and implementation of technologies that can help combat illegal fishing and protect our oceans.

By raising awareness, demanding change, and supporting innovative solutions like My Stealth Runner, we can help ensure a healthy ocean and a secure future for fisherfolk around the world.

Discover more from WPS News
Subscribe to get the latest posts sent to your email.

Remembering 9/11: A Day of Unimaginable Horror and Resilience

A Day That Changed the World: The 9/11 Attacks

September 11th, 2001 is a date etched into the minds of millions around the globe. It was a day of unimaginable horror, a day that forever altered the course of history.

The events of that fateful morning unfolded in a series of coordinated terrorist attacks orchestrated by the Islamic extremist group al-Qaeda. Nineteen hijackers, armed with box cutters, seized control of four commercial airplanes. Two of these planes were flown into the Twin Towers of the World Trade Center in New York City, causing them to collapse. A third plane struck the Pentagon in Washington, D.C., while a fourth crashed into a field in Shanksville, Pennsylvania, after passengers attempted to regain control of the aircraft.

The attacks resulted in the deaths of nearly 3,000 people, including firefighters, police officers, and civilians from all walks of life. The devastation caused by the attacks was immense, both physically and emotionally. The iconic skyline of New York City was forever changed, and the nation was plunged into a state of shock and grief.

In the aftermath of the attacks, the United States launched a global war on terrorism, targeting al-Qaeda and other extremist groups. The country's foreign policy and national security priorities were dramatically reshaped, with a focus on intelligence gathering, homeland security, and military intervention.

The 9/11 attacks continue to have a profound impact on the world. They serve as a stark reminder of the fragility of human life and the dangers of extremism. The attacks also sparked important conversations about global security, international cooperation, and the role of religion in society.

As we commemorate the anniversary of September 11th, let us remember the victims of this tragedy and honor their memory. Let us also strive to build a world free from violence and hatred, where peace and understanding prevail.

Discover more from WPS News
Subscribe to get the latest posts sent to your email.

I'll Rejoice: A Slam Poem

In the land of vibrant sun and sea,
A soul yearns to break free,
From the chains of stagnation and despair,
To rise above, to breathe in the fresh air.

Lost in the maze of life's cruel game,
Struggling against the current, against the flame,
Living on the edge, teetering on the brink,
Desperate for change, to find a new link.

I refuse to conform, to play their game,
I won't be a puppet in their twisted frame,
I bring gifts to the table, unique and bright,
I deserve to be valued, in the spotlight.

I won't be a cog in their heartless machine,
I won't let them crush me, unseen,
I want justice for the pain they've caused,
For the dreams they've shattered, the lives they've paused.

I know there's more, a missing key,
To unlock the door, to set me free,
I'll keep searching, I'll keep fighting,
For a future where I'm truly thriving.

So listen up, you callous few,
Your time will come, your deeds will undo,
I'll rise above, I'll find my way,
And in the end, I'll have my say.

I am strong, I am fierce, I am bold,
I'll write my story, in letters of gold,
I'll find my path, I'll make my mark,
And in the end, I'll light up the dark.

So watch out world, here I come,
A force to be reckoned with, a beating drum,
I'll find my purpose, I'll find my voice,

And in the end, I'll rejoice.

A Sea of Uncertainty: Filipino Fishermen Face Peril

The vast expanse of the West Philippine Sea (WPS) offers a bounty for Filipino fishermen, but lately, it's become a place of increasing peril. Recent events highlight the complex challenges faced by those who work these waters.

In late April, news broke of Filipino fisherfolk being harassed by Chinese Coast Guard (CCG) ships while setting up fishing gear at Recto Bank. This wasn't an isolated incident. Just a month later, reports surfaced of missing "payaos" (fish aggregating devices) belonging to fishermen in the Scarborough Shoal.

These events come amidst escalating tensions in the WPS. China's territorial claims often clash with those of the Philippines, leading to disputes over fishing rights and maritime resources. The presence of Chinese vessels can be intimidating for Filipino fishermen, hindering their ability to work freely in their own traditional fishing grounds.

Just a few weeks ago, tragedy struck. A fishing boat explosion near Bajo de Masinloc left two Filipino fishermen injured. Thankfully, the Philippine Coast Guard (PCG) conducted a successful rescue operation. Notably, the PCG also reported sighting Chinese vessels in the vicinity.

The co-existence of these events paints a worrying picture. Filipino fishermen face not only the natural dangers of the sea but also the uncertainty created by the political climate. Harassment, missing equipment, and now, a boat explosion – the fear of venturing out to earn a living must be immense.

The resilience of Filipino fishermen is undeniable. They continue to put food on tables despite the risks. However, the question remains: for how long can they continue to operate under such pressure?

The need for a peaceful resolution to the territorial disputes in the WPS is paramount. Filipino fishermen deserve the right to work safely in their own waters. Until then, the sea remains a place of both bounty and uncertainty.

This is where the Stealth Runner project is designed to help. We are a team dedicated to ensuring the safety and security of Filipino fishermen in the WPS. If you are a skilled sailor who thrives in challenging environments, consider joining our crew. Together, we can navigate these uncertain waters and protect the livelihood of our fellow Filipinos.

Help Us Build a Brighter Future for the West Philippine Sea!

The Stealth Runner project relies on the support of passionate individuals like you. Your contributions, big or small, can make a real difference. Here's how you can get involved:

- Donate: Every dollar helps us build and equip these essential vessels. Visit our donation page at patreon.com/AllenGuadalupe
- Spread the Word: Share our story on social media, tell your friends and family, and help us raise awareness about the Stealth Runner project.
- Volunteer Your Skills: We're always looking for talented individuals to join our team. Whether you have marketing expertise, nautical experience, or simply a passion for helping others, we welcome your contribution.
- Join the Crew: Are you a skilled mariner who wants to make a positive impact? We're building a team to operate the Stealth Runner fleet.

Together, we can empower Filipino fisherfolk, protect the marine environment, and ensure a sustainable future for the West Philippine Sea. Let's make a wave of change!

Discover more from WPS News
Subscribe to get the latest posts sent to your email.

PT Boats: Tiny Terrors of the Pacific War!

… and the Stealth Runner's Modern Mission.

Have you ever heard of David vs. Goliath? Well, in World War II, the Pacific Ocean became a giant battlefield, and the US Navy had a secret weapon: PT boats! These weren't your grandpa's fishing boats. Imagine a miniature warship, lightning fast and packed with a punch.

These boats, about the size of a school bus, were armed with torpedoes (underwater missiles), machine guns, and depth charges (underwater bombs). Their job? To sneak up on HUGE enemy ships and unleash a surprise attack before anyone knew what hit them!

Think of them as ninjas of the sea. They were quiet, agile, and could dart in and out of danger zones faster than the enemy could even aim their guns. PT boats were perfect for:

- Surprise Attacks: They'd zip up to enemy ships, launch their torpedoes, and disappear before the enemy could even fire back!
- Protecting Allies: They acted like bodyguards for bigger, slower ships, chasing away any enemy threats.
- Secret Missions: They'd sneak behind enemy lines to rescue soldiers or gather intel (secret information) about enemy plans.
- Island Hopping: They helped soldiers land on enemy islands by clearing the way and providing backup fire.

PT boat crews were some of the bravest sailors in the war. They faced huge dangers in tiny boats, but their daring tactics helped turn the tide in the Pacific.

Now, this might make you think of another cool story – the Flying Tigers! These were American pilots who fought for China before the US entered World War II. Just like the Flying Tigers helped a friend in need, could PT boats be used again someday?

Enter the Stealth Runner! Inspired by the spirit of the PT boats, the Stealth Runner is a modern take on that same idea. It's a specially designed Filipino boat, built with local materials to be quiet and maneuverable. Imagine it as a guardian angel for Filipino fisherfolk in the West Philippine Sea.

Just like the PT boats, the Stealth Runner is:

- Silent but Deadly: Its quiet engine allows it to approach fish without scaring them away, helping the fisherfolk have a better catch.

- A Protector: It can help ensure the safety of fisherfolk on the high seas, keeping an eye out for trouble.
- A Friend in Need: It can offer assistance in case of emergencies, like bad weather or equipment problems.

The Stealth Runner might be smaller than some other boats, but it has a big heart. It's all about helping hardworking fisherfolk and protecting the vital resources of the West Philippine Sea.

So, the next time you hear about the brave PT boats, remember the Stealth Runner too! They both show that even the smallest warriors can have a giant impact!

Help Us Build a Brighter Future for the West Philippine Sea!

The Stealth Runner project relies on the support of passionate individuals like you. Your contributions, big or small, can make a real difference. Here's how you can get involved:

- Donate: Every dollar helps us build and equip these essential vessels. Visit our donation page at patreon.com/AllenGuadalupe
- Spread the Word: Share our story on social media, tell your friends and family, and help us raise awareness about the Stealth Runner project.
- Volunteer Your Skills: We're always looking for talented individuals to join our team. Whether you have marketing expertise, nautical experience, or simply a passion for helping others, we welcome your contribution.
- Join the Crew: Are you a skilled mariner who wants to make a positive impact? We're building a team to operate the Stealth Runner fleet.

Together, we can empower Filipino fisherfolk, protect the marine environment, and ensure a sustainable future for the West Philippine Sea. Let's make a wave of change!

Discover more from WPS News
Subscribe to get the latest posts sent to your email.

Life in 2027: A Vision of the Future

This essay was written in 2004, and was part of my first book SpiritFlight. The point it was to make is that we do not have to fear the future, and predictions about the future are not necessarily psychic, or religious in nature. They are just based on past events. If you know the past you have a pretty good idea of what will come in the future. Perhaps it should be 2037, but, you will get my point.

I have selected 2027 as the year when the future starts. What I mean is that the year 2027 will be the year when the next cycle of prosperity begins. One such era began in 1945. Twenty years later began a time of spirituality. The next phase of the cycle, the age of the individual, started in 1983. The next crisis cycle began in 2001. This crisis cycle should be resolved by 2019. Given a few years to clean up the debris, by 2027, we should have another time of prosperity.

The world that will exist in 2027 will be as different as 1953 was from 1929. 1929 was the beginning of the last crisis cycle. As frightening as these times of crisis are, humankind has survived them all. The next will be no different. There are over three hundred million Americans alive today. Even if our eight largest cities were attacked with nuclear weapons, our losses would be only about forty million Americans. Of course, that would be unspeakably awful; however, two hundred and sixty million Americans would survive. No doubt, these survivors will redefine the nation and the world.

These survivors will rise from the ashes demanding balance. The "extreme" philosophy of Generation X will be passé. The thrill of the extreme will die with the real hardships faced during the crisis. The result will be moderation in all things. Reason will return to the political landscape. Social responsibility will return to the forefront, and the corporate monopolies that now rule will give way to the common good.

Technology will be used to improve life. Streets and highways, neglected in favor of weapons expenditures, will be rebuilt with the future in mind. They will use computer technology to be smarter and safer. Artificial intelligence will drive your vehicle for you by means of expert sensors and global positioning systems.

Newspapers will be electronic as publishers finally wrestle the internet away from individual mavericks. They will be tailored to your interests. Audio and video will digitally stream to your vehicle as corporate radio and television now do.

Wages will finally climb to reasonable levels. Money itself will be adjusted in value. Paper money will become more and more novel as debit cards become more popular. In order to ensure security, some form of biometrics will be utilized for debit cards, most likely an electronic thumbprint.

Two factors will increase the average income. One is diminished population levels forcing a more competitive wage structure. The second factor will be a sense of social responsibility redefining what is reasonable profit while rewarding workers for their efforts. This will be forced by revitalized unionization.

Credit as we understand it will disappear. The unsecured loan will be held in disdain by consumers and businesses alike. This will be a result of the overuse of credit scores for non-credit purposes and the irresponsible use of credit in the previous two generations.

Health care will finally get the attention it deserves. The new social contract will elevate health care to a right. In the aftermath of an outbreak of a biological pathogen, some form of socialized medicine will emerge. If not, otherwise healthy people will succumb to treatable diseases for lack of adequate insurance. Those uninsured and underinsured will suffer economic hardship due to the high cost of health care. This will be followed by the collapse of a health insurance industry unable to pay the claims of millions of covered patients in the wake of the epidemic. The government will relieve the private health insurance companies of their responsibilities and will evolve an effective and efficient health care system.

The medical community itself will undergo change. Society will see it as partially culpable for the crisis. It will carry a sense of guilt for its inability to render aid in the early stages of the outbreak. Health care professionals will be forced to restructure medical care to be responsive to all people.

Cost effective and efficient desalinization will provide additional sources of fresh water and allow resources to be diverted back into agriculture.

The division between rural and urban will blur. Small towns will be revitalized as survivors scatter across the country. Cities that survive will be far less populated. Corporate America, fearing the target created by building in clusters, will disperse. Smaller cities will expand in size to accommodate the new influx of business and people. The government will intervene to set fair market values for real estate to prevent price gouging. Super cities like New York, Chicago, and Los Angeles, having been abandoned during the crisis, will be recovered as living monuments to the twentieth century.

Multinational corporations will cease to exist by this time. In the year 2027, distrust of foreign influence and the inability of the multinationals to respond to national interests will finally take their toll on these corporations. The market will de-invest in the global giants in favor of more localized firms. Production facilities will be forced back into the United States.

The classic conservative values of God, home, community, and employer will prevail in the surviving culture, at least in publicly. In private, neo-hedonistic subcultures will add a diversion to the publicly uniform life. Monogamous marriages for public show will provide cover for discreet extramarital affairs. Indiscretion will be socially punished, but forgotten and forgiven quickly as long as the primary family unit remains in tact and the children are not affected.

Children will be treasured, pampered, and protected as national treasures. The crisis will assert a sense of the fragility of life and the blessing of existence. Certain side effects of the crisis will result in sterilization. Couples will be free to adopt orphans and unsupported children. Every child will be viewed as a community asset; the community will come to the aid of any struggling parent. Parents will be held in high esteem for having children and will readily find support with any issue. Community and social responsibility will connect with individual responsibility to provide an artificially safe environment in the surviving nation.

Religion will find itself delegated to private life. It will no longer be a viable political tool. By consensus, religion in public life will be suspect. The surviving generation will not tolerate religious bigotry, public displays of religion outside of acceptable religious centers or group identification based on religion.

The surviving generation will demand order from the religious and anti-religious factions. The same holds true concerning political divisions. Wide political divergences will be tolerated only as long as they remain in the confines of political aspirations.

National politics will be defined by the overwhelming, almost compulsive desire to achieve diplomatic resolutions to all problems. Elected officials will be skilled political leaders and diplomats. Armed conflict will be repulsive to the surviving generation. They will engage the world on all levels to find common communal values and build solutions.

If not replaced, the United Nations will become a form of elected representative global government. It will function on a parliamentary system similar to the British system. This body will be a two-house body, much like the United States Congress. One house will be based on population while the other will allow for equal representation. The executive branch of the new United Nations will have police powers. The surviving generation will demand that national sovereignty take a back seat to global necessities. Any national government that opposes this trend will be replaced. We will demand global engagement to ensure global social order. The key for the traumatized surviving generation will be order. They will demand it, and they will get it.

The trauma of the crisis will have a prolonged effect on its survivors. Drug use will be high due to traumatized survivors self-medicating and to the early failures of the medical community to cope with the impact of high casualties during the crisis. The result will be the decriminalization of drug use and a surviving generation demanding solutions to drug dependence. Drug use will be stripped of its social stigma and addressed as a medical issue. All forms of abnormal behavior due to delayed stress will be addressed through the medical community.

As the surviving generation gives way to the treasured generation, uniformity and pragmatism will give way to nonconformity and the exploration of individual expression. Creativity will rise in the arts and the media and pave the way towards an enlightened, educated era of free expression.

These are just predictions based on the events of history. History is only a guide; it is not a dictator. We may not be able to avert the crisis. However, we can minimize it by rationally addressing it. Our job now is to make sure that people survive to see the next era of prosperity. Our future is bright; we just need to get there.

Discover more from WPS News
Subscribe to get the latest posts sent to your email.

Blending Experience and Technology: Harnessing Open Source Intelligence for a Safer Tomorrow
Scattered Puzzle pieces waiting for the right person to put them all together.

OSINT

In the realm of intelligence gathering and analysis, the convergence of experience and technology has birthed a new frontier: Open Source Intelligence (OSINT) Gathering and Analytics. For one individual, the journey from a career in Uniformed Contract Security to pioneering in this domain represents a blend of lifelong expertise and a profound passion for advocacy.

Security & Technology

Having navigated the waters of Uniformed Contract Security and immersed in cutting-edge technologies since the 1990s, the decision to merge these skill sets post-retirement was a natural evolution. The transition into Open Source Intelligence was not just a career pivot but a transformation into a realm where information harvested from publicly available sources on the Internet and news platforms becomes a treasure trove for analysis. By applying the intricate blend of science and art to decipher the 'what,' 'why,' and 'what next,' this individual's approach stands out for its fresh perspective and a commitment to minimal confirmation bias.

Tilt the Scales

In a world perpetually perched on the edge of uncertainty, the ability to sieve through vast volumes of data and proactively anticipate potential disruptions is paramount. As rightly emphasized, having advanced notification of critical junctures can tilt the scale from manageable losses to catastrophic consequences. The key to maintaining accuracy lies in unwaveringly anchoring insights to source data, while reliability is fortified by a rigorous vetting process of sources. It is through this tenacious dedication to detail that foresight transcends the realm of impossibility.

Foresight

The foresight displayed in predicting the '07/'08 Great Recession, against conventional skepticism, underscores the visionary approach embedded in the fabric of this business. The adage that the future is the only predictable facet in a predominantly reactive Cybersecurity landscape resonates profoundly. As the digital realm becomes increasingly fraught with unforeseen challenges, the role of Open Source Intelligence emerges as a beacon of light—illuminating pathways to preemptive action and strategic resilience.

The Tangible Reality

In conclusion, the fusion of seasoned experience from the security domain with a fervent embrace of emerging technologies has propelled the narrative of Open Source Intelligence

Gathering and Analytics into uncharted territories of innovation. As this visionary entrepreneur navigates this dynamic landscape with a keen eye on the horizon, the promise of a safer tomorrow, underpinned by empirical insights and proactive measures, becomes not just a possibility but a tangible reality.

Your expertise and commitment to the realm of Open Source Intelligence bring a unique perspective that promises to shape the future of cybersecurity and intelligence analysis.

Regimentation
I would highly recommend considering Cliff Potts as an additional intelligence asset to any operation. Their exceptional abilities and knowledge would undoubtedly be a valuable addition to the team.

Do What You Love. Love What You Do.
Open Source Intelligence
Discover more from WPS News
Subscribe to get the latest posts sent to your email.

The Evolution of Journalism: Embracing AI for Information Dissemination

AI-Powered News: A New Era of Information Dissemination
By Cliff Potts

As a seasoned writer who has spent years crafting narratives, I've noticed a shift in my own writing habits. While I still contribute significantly to my work, I've increasingly turned to AI to assist in generating content, particularly for my news platform, WPS News.

This transition isn't a departure from my commitment to quality journalism. Instead, it's a strategic adaptation to the evolving landscape of information consumption. AI tools have become indispensable in keeping up with the rapid pace of current events and ensuring that our readers have access to the most up-to-date information.

One of the primary benefits of AI-generated content is its ability to streamline the research process. By analyzing vast amounts of data, AI can quickly identify relevant trends, uncover hidden patterns, and provide valuable insights that might otherwise be missed. This allows me to focus on crafting compelling narratives and ensuring that the information we share is accurate and informative.

However, it's important to acknowledge that AI is not a substitute for human judgment. While it can be a powerful tool, it's essential to use it critically and responsibly. The human element remains crucial in ensuring that the content we produce is relevant, engaging, and aligned with our editorial values.

As we continue to navigate the complexities of the digital age, it's clear that AI will play an increasingly important role in shaping the way we consume and share information. By embracing this technology while maintaining a strong commitment to journalistic integrity, we can create a more informed and engaged society.

Join us at WPS News for the latest updates and insights. Subscribe to our newsletter, follow us on X (@cliffpotts, @chi_ship), and share our content with your network. Together, we can build a brighter future.

Discover more from WPS News
Subscribe to get the latest posts sent to your email.

Lessons from Lani: The Intersection of Politics, Religion, and the Collapse of Occupy

Lani, a captivating individual with great stage presence, was once a supervisor at Addison Apple, although not directly overseeing Allen Guadalupe. Known for her beauty and ability to command attention in group settings, she had a particular fondness for blue jeans. Allen Guadalupe recounts a valuable lesson learned from Lani that sheds light on the collapse of the Occupy movement on a global scale.

Reflecting on the advice passed down from previous generations to avoid discussions on politics and religion, Lani shared her mother's admonition against engaging in these topics. The ethos of maintaining peace and harmony within the household, prevalent among the GI and Silent generations post-World War II, was ingrained in both Lani and Allen Guadalupe. However, Allen Guadalupe, a latchkey kid of earlier times, found himself delving into these forbidden territories in search of his identity.

The narrative shifts to the era from the aftermath of the Vietnam War until the present day, where religion and politics dominate the conversations of Baby Boomers and Generation X, albeit with differing perspectives. Fast forward to 2011, the year of the Occupy Movement, a global initiative advocating for political and income equality. While the movement primarily focused on political discourse, religion was either brushed aside or met with disdain, leading to its eventual downfall.

Allen Guadalupe posits that the failure of Occupy can be attributed to its neglect of the intersection between politics and religion. By prioritizing diverse political ideologies while disregarding or disrespecting religious beliefs, the movement alienated potential allies and supporters. The relentless emphasis on political activism, epitomized by the slogan "Occupy Wall Street," overshadowed the need for a more inclusive and holistic approach.

Moreover, the author underscores the intense frustration and anger that fueled the Occupy Movement. It served as a cathartic release of pent-up grievances against the corporate takeover of the American political process. As Xers, Millennials, and Gen Z individuals mobilized against the perceived failures of the system, the movement evolved from coalition-building to a visceral outpouring of discontent.

After the initial months, Occupy lost its focus on collaboration and shifted towards expressing raw emotion and outrage. The growing sentiment of business entities being "too big to fail" and individuals being deemed expendable underscored the societal disillusionment that permeated the movement. Even the Obama administration, once seen as a beacon of hope, faced scrutiny for its ties to mega banks, further fueling public discontent.

The author highlights the challenges faced by Occupy activists, including police crackdowns on peaceful protests and a media narrative that often sensationalized or misrepresented their efforts. Despite the movement's ultimate collapse, the legacy of Occupy serves as a reminder of the power of grassroots mobilization and the complexities inherent in navigating the intersection of politics, religion, and societal change.

In conclusion, Allen Guadalupe's reflections on Lani's wisdom offer valuable insights into the multifaceted dynamics that shaped the Occupy Movement. By acknowledging the interconnected nature of political activism, religious discourse, and social upheaval, individuals can strive for a more inclusive and sustainable approach to effecting meaningful change in society.

Today marks the 13th Anniversary of Occupy Wall Street .

Occupy Wall Street (OWS) was a left-wing populist movement against economic inequality, corporate greed, big finance, and the influence of money in politics that began in Zuccotti Park, located in New York City's Financial District, and lasted for fifty-nine days—from September 17 to November 15, 2011.[1]

The Occupy movement was an international populist socio-political movement that expressed opposition to social and economic inequality and to the perceived lack of real democracy around the world.[2]

Discover more from WPS News
Subscribe to get the latest posts sent to your email.

---

[1] Wikipedia contributors, "Occupy Wall Street," Wikipedia, The Free Encyclopedia, https://en.wikipedia.org/w/index.php?title=Occupy_Wall_Street&oldid=1227841294 (accessed June 18, 2024).

[2] Wikipedia contributors, "Occupy movement," Wikipedia, The Free Encyclopedia, https://en.wikipedia.org/w/index.php?title=Occupy_movement&oldid=1228004865 (accessed June 18, 2024).

The Mukden Incident: Unraveling the Japanese Invasion of Manchuria (1931)

Introduction:

In the annals of history, certain events stand out as pivotal moments that shape the course of nations and regions. One such event is the Japanese invasion of Manchuria in 1931, also known as the Mukden Incident. This surprise attack by the Imperial Japanese Army against Chinese forces not only marked the beginning of a broader conflict in the region but also had far-reaching consequences that reverberated across the globe.

The Mukden Incident:

On September 18, 1931, a section of the South Manchurian Railway near Mukden (now Shenyang) was dynamited by Japanese soldiers, who then blamed Chinese dissidents for the attack. This false pretext provided the justification for the Japanese military to launch a full-scale invasion of Manchuria, a resource-rich region in northeastern China.

The invasion was swift and decisive, with Japanese forces quickly overwhelming Chinese defenders. Within a matter of months, the Japanese had seized control of key cities and strategic locations in Manchuria, establishing a puppet state known as Manchukuo with the last Qing emperor, Puyi, installed as a figurehead ruler.

International Response:

The Japanese invasion of Manchuria sent shockwaves through the international community. The League of Nations, the precursor to the United Nations, launched an investigation into the incident and condemned Japan's actions. However, the League's response was largely toothless, as major powers like Britain, France, and the United States were preoccupied with their own economic concerns and reluctant to take strong action against Japan.

Consequences:

The Japanese invasion of Manchuria had profound consequences for the region and the world at large. It marked the beginning of Japan's aggressive expansionist policies in Asia, leading to further conflicts and ultimately culminating in World War II. The failure of the international community to effectively respond to Japan's actions in Manchuria also exposed the limitations of collective security arrangements and set a dangerous precedent for future acts of aggression.

Legacy:

The legacy of the Mukden Incident continues to resonate today, serving as a cautionary tale about the dangers of unchecked militarism and the importance of upholding the principles of international law and diplomacy. The events of 1931 remind us of the need for vigilance in the face of aggression and the imperative of fostering cooperation and dialogue to prevent conflict and promote peace.

Conclusion:

The Japanese invasion of Manchuria in 1931 stands as a stark reminder of the consequences of unchecked aggression and the challenges of maintaining peace and stability in a rapidly changing world. As we reflect on this dark chapter in history, let us strive to learn from the mistakes of the past and work together to build a future founded on justice, cooperation, and mutual respect.

Discover more from WPS News
Subscribe to get the latest posts sent to your email.

The Modern Balangay: Safeguarding Filipino Fisherfolk in the West Philippine Sea

The Stealth Runner Project Safeguarding Filipino Fisherfolk

Across the vast expanse of the Pacific Ocean, a new kind of vessel carves its path through the waves. The Stealth Runner project, inspired by the rich maritime history of the Philippines, is building a fleet of modern balangays – patrol boats designed to safeguard Filipino fisherfolk in the West Philippine Sea.

The balangay, a traditional Filipino double outrigger canoe, was once a symbol of daring exploration and skilled seafaring. Today, the Stealth Runner project reimagines this legacy with a 21st-century twist.

Challenges at Sea:

Filipino fisherfolk, the backbone of the country's seafood industry, face a multitude of challenges on the high seas. They contend with overfishing, illegal fishing practices by foreign vessels, and the constant threat of piracy. These challenges not only endanger their livelihoods, but also threaten the delicate marine ecosystems of the West Philippine Sea.

A Modern Guardian:

The Stealth Runner is more than just a boat; it's a beacon of hope for Filipino fisherfolk. Built with locally sourced, sustainable wood, this innovative vessel is designed to be quiet and maneuverable. Its silent engine allows it to approach fish without spooking them, promoting sustainable fishing practices.

Strength in Tradition and Technology:

The Stealth Runner embodies the Filipino spirit of resourcefulness. It combines traditional knowledge of boat building with modern technology to create a powerful tool for protecting the seas and its people. The use of local wood not only provides a sustainable solution, but also connects the project to the Philippines' rich maritime heritage.

Safeguarding a Future:

The Stealth Runner Project is not just about protecting the present; it's about safeguarding a future where Filipino fisherfolk can thrive. By providing them with support and security, the project empowers them to continue their essential work while ensuring the sustainability of the marine environment.

The story of the Stealth Runner is a testament to Filipino ingenuity and resilience. It's a modern balangay, a protector carves its way through the waves, not just for the sake of the fisherfolk, but for the future of the Philippines and its precious maritime heritage.

Join the Movement:

The Stealth Runner project relies on the support of passionate individuals like you. Visit our website to learn more about how you can contribute to a brighter future for the West Philippine Sea and the Filipino fisherfolk who depend on it.

Help Us Build a Brighter Future for the West Philippine Sea!

The Stealth Runner project relies on the support of passionate individuals like you. Your contributions, big or small, can make a real difference. Here's how you can get involved:

- Donate: Every dollar helps us build and equip these essential vessels. Visit our donation page at patreon.com/AllenGuadalupe
- Spread the Word: Share our story on social media, tell your friends and family, and help us raise awareness about the Stealth Runner project.
- Volunteer Your Skills: We're always looking for talented individuals to join our team. Whether you have marketing expertise, nautical experience, or simply a passion for helping others, we welcome your contribution.
- Join the Crew: Are you a skilled mariner who wants to make a positive impact? We're building a team to operate the Stealth Runner fleet.

Together, we can empower Filipino fisherfolk, protect the marine environment, and ensure a sustainable future for the West Philippine Sea. Let's make a wave of change!

Discover more from WPS News
Subscribe to get the latest posts sent to your email.

Empowering Filipino Fisherfolk:
The Stealth Runner Project

How the Stealth Runner Project Promotes Sustainable Fishing in the West Philippine Sea

The West Philippine Sea, a vast expanse of turquoise waters teeming with life, faces a growing threat. Overfishing and illegal fishing practices by foreign vessels are disrupting the delicate balance of this marine paradise. These unsustainable practices not only deplete fish stocks, but also harm coral reefs and other fragile ecosystems.

A Silent Threat to a Fragile Ecosystem:

Oversized fishing trawlers often use loud engines and destructive nets, scraping the seabed and causing widespread damage. This disrupts fish breeding grounds and destroys vital habitats for countless marine species. The consequences are dire – dwindling fish populations, damaged coral reefs, and a disrupted marine food chain.

Enter the Stealth Runner: A Guardian of the Sea

The Stealth Runner project emerges as a beacon of hope in this troubled paradise. These innovative patrol boats, inspired by the ingenuity of Filipino boatbuilders, are designed with sustainability in mind.

Built for a Greener Future:

- Silent Guardians: The Stealth Runner's quiet engine allows it to approach fish without spooking them. This promotes the use of traditional fishing methods that rely on skill and knowledge, rather than loud machinery and disruptive techniques.
- Locally Sourced, Eco-Friendly Materials: Built with local, sustainable wood, the Stealth Runner minimizes its environmental footprint. This approach not only reduces reliance on imported materials, but also showcases the potential for eco-friendly solutions within the Philippines.

Empowering Filipino Fisherfolk for a Sustainable Future:

The heart of the Stealth Runner project lies in empowering Filipino fisherfolk to become stewards of the West Philippine Sea.

- Sustainable Fishing Practices: By working alongside fisherfolk, the Stealth Runner crew can educate them about sustainable fishing methods and responsible resource management.
- Protecting Livelihoods: The Stealth Runner acts as a deterrent against illegal fishing practices, safeguarding the fish stocks that Filipino fisherfolk rely on for their livelihoods.

The Stealth Runner Needs Your Support:

The fight to protect the West Philippine Sea and its precious ecosystems is an ongoing battle. Donations are crucial to building and maintaining the Stealth Runner fleet, ensuring a continued presence in these vulnerable waters.

By supporting the Stealth Runner project, you're not just contributing to a greener future for the West Philippine Sea; you're empowering Filipino fisherfolk and safeguarding a vital source of food and income for generations to come.

Visit our website today to learn more about how you can donate and become a part of the solution!

Discover more from WPS News
Subscribe to get the latest posts sent to your email.

Nuclear Threat in the South China Sea: A Philippine Perspective

A Potential Nuclear Showdown in the South China Sea: Implications for the Philippines
By WPS News Staff

A recent analysis by Elizabeth Suh, a research associate at the German Institute for Foreign and Security Affairs, has raised concerns about the potential for a nuclear escalation in the South China Sea. Suh suggests that while the US may not use nuclear weapons to defend the Philippines, a direct conflict between China and the US could lead to such a scenario.

The Philippines, a non-nuclear state, is caught in the middle of the ongoing geopolitical tensions between the two superpowers. The potential for a nuclear conflict in the region has serious implications for the country's security and economic stability.

While the possibility of a nuclear exchange may seem remote, it is essential to consider the potential consequences. Such an event could have catastrophic effects on the environment, human health, and the global economy.

Key Considerations:

- Geopolitical Tensions: The ongoing territorial disputes in the South China Sea, coupled with the increasing military presence of both the US and China, have heightened tensions in the region.
- Nuclear Proliferation: The risk of nuclear proliferation in the region is also a concern. If any of the countries in the region were to acquire nuclear weapons, it could further destabilize the situation.
- Economic Impacts: A nuclear conflict would have devastating economic consequences for the Philippines, as well as for the global economy.

Conclusion:

While the likelihood of a nuclear conflict in the South China Sea remains uncertain, it is crucial for the Philippines to be prepared for such a scenario. The country must continue to pursue diplomatic efforts to de-escalate tensions and promote regional stability. Additionally, the Philippines should invest in civil defense and emergency preparedness measures to mitigate the potential impacts of a nuclear conflict.

Source: Chi, Cristina. How a US-China nuclear showdown threatens the Philippines, PhilStar Global , 19 Sept. 2024, www.philstar.com/headlines/2024/09/19/2386441/how-us-china-nuclear-showdown-threatens-philippines.

Discover more from WPS News
Subscribe to get the latest posts sent to your email.

Significance of the Autumnal Equinox in Mabon

Mabon (MAY-bone or MAH-bawn) is named for the Welsh God and it is seen as the second of the three harvests, and particularly as a celebration of the vine harvests and of wine. It is also associated with apples as symbols of life renewed.

Celebrating new-made wine, harvesting apples and vine products, and visiting burial cairns to place an apple upon them, were all ways in which the Celts honored this Sabbat. (Avalon, one of the many Celtic names for the Land of the Dead, literally means the "land of apples".) These acts symbolized both thankfulness for the life-giving harvest, and the wish of the living to be reunited with their dead.

Taken from "Celtic Myth and Magick" by Edain McCoy

Sweater weather is upon us. The beginning of the autumn season marks the end of warm summer days and the start of longer chilly nights.

On Sunday, September 22, 2024 We Celebrate the Autumnal Equinox- But What is That?

The fall equinox and the first day of autumn arrives on Sunday, September 22, 2024, at 08:44 A.M. EDT in the Northern Hemisphere. The equinox occurs at the same moment worldwide.

When Is the First Day of Fall? The Autumnal Equinox.

Discover more from WPS News
Subscribe to get the latest posts sent to your email.

China's Crackdown on Foreign Businesses Explained

No One is Safe in China, China Uncensored

This video is about the current situation in China. It covers a variety of topics, including the Chinese government's crackdown on foreign businesses, the targeting of Chinese citizens by scammers, and the increasing tensions between China and other countries.

The Chinese government is making it increasingly difficult for foreign businesses to operate in China. In 2023, a record low of 66% of foreign companies were profitable in China. This is due to a number of factors, including the Chinese government's increasingly hostile attitude towards foreign businesses, the slowing Chinese economy, and the increasing tensions between China and other countries.

Chinese citizens are also being targeted by scammers. A recent case involved a Chinese crime syndicate that was operating out of the UK. The scammers used a method known as "pig butchering" to lure their victims into making large investments. The scammers eventually stole an estimated $5.3 million from their victims.

The tensions between China and other countries are also on the rise. In recent months, China has increased its military activity in the South China Sea and has threatened to invade Taiwan. The United States and other Western countries have condemned China's actions and have called for it to stop its aggression.

This video provides a comprehensive overview of the current situation in China. It is a must-read for anyone who wants to learn more about this important topic.

South China Sea Crisis: Chinese Fishing Boats, Manned by Soldiers, Face Philippine Counterattacks

This video is about the escalating tensions in the South China Sea between China and the Philippines. The Philippines has taken a firm stance against China's aggression in the disputed waters, vowing to defend its Coast Guard vessel BRP Teresa Magbanua at all costs. China has been sending large numbers of fishing vessels to the area, crowding the waters and setting new records for the year. These fishing vessels are not ordinary fishing boats, but are disguised military tools. They are used to gather intelligence, assert China's presence, and even cause trouble by ramming other ships or engaging in standoffs. The Philippines is considering using their fishing boats to bring fuel on board the BRP Teresa Magbanua, which is running low on fuel. The US military is concerned about China's Maritime militia, and has been collecting data on their activities. The US military believes that these militia ships are a threat to regional stability, and that they could be used in a future conflict.

China rams Philippine ship while 60 Minutes on board; South China Sea tensions could draw U.S. in

This video segment from 60 Minutes focuses on the increasing tensions between China and the Philippines in the South China Sea. The Philippines has exclusive economic rights in the area, but China claims almost all of the South China Sea. This has led to a number of confrontations between the two countries, including the recent ramming of a Philippine Coast Guard ship by a Chinese vessel. The United States has a mutual defense treaty with the Philippines, which could mean American intervention if the conflict escalates.

Some key points from the video:

- The Philippines has exclusive economic rights in the South China Sea, but China claims almost all of the area.
- This has led to a number of confrontations between the two countries, including the recent ramming of a Philippine Coast Guard ship by a Chinese vessel.
- The United States has a mutual defense treaty with the Philippines, which could mean American intervention if the conflict escalates.
- The Philippines is concerned that China may try to take control of Sabina Shoal, a disputed area in the South China Sea.
- China has been using tactics just short of war to assert its claims in the South China Sea.
- The United States has condemned China for its actions and has committed to supporting the Philippines.
- The video concludes with a warning that the conflict between China and the Philippines could escalate into a wider war.

Discover more from WPS News
Subscribe to get the latest posts sent to your email.

The Ethical Dilemma of Doing Business in China

The Corporate Conundrum: China's Allure and Western Disregard

The intricate dance between multinational corporations and China has become a defining feature of the 21st century global economy. While Western nations grapple with concerns over human rights, intellectual property theft, and geopolitical tensions, many corporations seem more than willing to overlook these issues in pursuit of profit. This phenomenon raises a critical question: why are so many multinational corporations so eager to appease China at the expense of Western values and interests?

One primary factor driving this trend is the sheer size and economic potential of the Chinese market. With a population of over 1.4 billion people and a rapidly growing middle class, China presents a lucrative opportunity for businesses seeking to expand their reach and increase revenue. The allure of such a vast consumer base can be overwhelming, prompting corporations to prioritize market access over ethical considerations.

Additionally, China's low labor costs and efficient manufacturing capabilities make it an attractive destination for production. By outsourcing manufacturing to China, companies can reduce costs and remain competitive in the global marketplace. This economic incentive can outweigh concerns about human rights abuses or unfair trade practices.

Moreover, the Chinese government has adopted policies that are designed to attract foreign investment. These policies include favorable tax rates, streamlined regulatory processes, and access to a skilled workforce. By offering such incentives, China has created a business environment that is highly appealing to multinational corporations.

However, the pursuit of profit in China comes at a cost. Human rights abuses, such as forced labor and the suppression of dissent, are well-documented in the country. Intellectual property theft is a pervasive problem, with Chinese companies often accused of stealing technology and violating patents. Furthermore, China's geopolitical ambitions, including its territorial claims in the South China Sea and its growing military power, pose a threat to regional stability and global security.

Despite these concerns, many multinational corporations continue to prioritize economic interests over ethical considerations. This is partly due to a lack of effective international regulations and enforcement mechanisms. While there are international organizations that seek to address human rights abuses and unfair trade practices, their power is limited.

In conclusion, the willingness of many multinational corporations to appease China can be attributed to a combination of factors, including the size of the Chinese market, economic incentives, and the favorable business environment created by the Chinese government. However, this approach comes at a cost, as it undermines Western values and interests. As the world grapples with the challenges posed by China's rise, it is imperative for corporations to adopt a more responsible and ethical approach to their business activities in the country.

Discover more from WPS News
Subscribe to get the latest posts sent to your email.

Navigating China's Maritime Changes: A U.S. Response

China's maritime strategy is evolving from gray-zone tactics to a more direct and aggressive approach, including using warships in confrontations. This shift is evident in the recent clashes at Second Thomas Shoal and the increased Chinese military activities with Russia. Experts believe that China is preparing its economy for potential blowback from this new approach. The Solomon Islands security pact is a sign of China's widening geographic focus in the Pacific. The United States needs to respond with a persistent naval presence and clear-eyed diplomacy, as demonstrated in the 2020 West Capella incident.

Source: Evolving "Grey Zone" Tactics: China's Maritime Grey Zone Tactics Are Evolving

America's Merchant Mariners: A Looming Shortage Threatens Our Economy and Security

The United States has a long and proud history as a maritime nation. Our merchant mariners have played a vital role in both peacetime and wartime, ensuring the flow of goods that keeps our economy humming and our nation secure. But today, the American maritime industry faces a serious challenge: a looming shortage of qualified mariners.

According to a recent article on gCaptain (U.S. Mariner Shortage Demands Action Now!), the mariner shortage is caused by a number of factors, including the aging of the current workforce, low awareness of maritime careers, and the demanding nature of the job. The consequences of this shortage could be severe. In peacetime, a shortage of mariners could lead to disruptions in the supply chain, driving up the cost of goods and services for American consumers. In wartime, a shortage of mariners could hinder our ability to project military power abroad.

What can be done to address the mariner shortage? The article suggests a number of solutions, including increased investment in maritime training programs, outreach to young people to raise awareness of maritime careers, and making the job of mariner more attractive by improving wages and working conditions.

The U.S. mariner shortage is a serious problem that demands immediate action. By taking steps to address the causes of the shortage, we can ensure that America's maritime industry continues to thrive for generations to come.

Source: U.S. Mariner Shortage Demands Action Now!

True Wealth: Embracing Convictions and Defying Tyranny

Many years ago, I arrived at the disheartening realization that attaining wealth in the traditional sense – the kind that would afford me the comfort to pursue my passions without fear of persecution or censure for simply being true to myself – was an elusive dream, a punishment of sorts. But punishment for what, you may wonder? It felt like a penalty for daring to engage in critical thinking, for daring to question the prevailing norms and challenge the popular beliefs held sacrosanct by the masses. The crime I was accused of? Exercising my intellect in a manner that deviated from the accepted illusions of the time.

For this transgression, I was subjected to a sentence of impoverishment, a form of exile from the realm of societal acceptance. And yet, despite the passage of time, the naked truth remains unchanged: the emperor, stripped of his fabricated garments of conformity and pretense, stands exposed before us, his illusions shattered by the unwavering light of critical inquiry.

As I muse on these thoughts on a languid Sunday afternoon, I am reminded that the pursuit of truth and authenticity often comes at a price, a cost that few are willing to bear. And yet, in the face of adversity and ostracism, I find solace in the knowledge that I have remained steadfast in my commitment to thinking critically, even when it meant standing alone against the tide of popular opinion.

The emperor may still be naked, but in his vulnerability lies the seed of liberation – a reminder that true wealth is not measured in material riches, but in the courage to embrace one's convictions and defy the tyranny of conformity.

Discover more from WPS News
Subscribe to get the latest posts sent to your email.

Join the Movement: Support the Stealth Runner Project Today

Safeguarding our Seas, Empowering our Kababayans

Kababayans abroad, a new wave of hope is rising in the West Philippine Sea. *The Stealth Runner project*, a testament to Filipino ingenuity, is building a fleet of innovative patrol boats designed to protect our fisherfolk and the vital marine resources they depend on.

A Growing Threat:

Overfishing, illegal fishing practices by foreign vessels, and piracy – these are the challenges Filipino fisherfolk face every day. These threats not only endanger their livelihoods, but also put a strain on the delicate marine ecosystems that sustain us all.

A Sustainable Solution:

The Stealth Runner project offers a beacon of hope in these troubled waters. These eco-friendly boats, built with locally sourced materials, boast silent engines that minimize disruption to marine life. This allows for more effective patrols and promotes responsible fishing practices.

More Than Just Protection:

The Stealth Runner project is about empowering Filipino fisherfolk to become stewards of the West Philippine Sea. By providing training and support, the project equips them with the knowledge and tools to operate more safely and sustainably.

How You Can Help:

As a Filipino expat, you can be a powerful voice for change. Here's how you can make a difference:

- **Amplify Our Voice:** Share the story of the Stealth Runner project on social media and with your communities. Raise awareness about the challenges faced by Filipino fisherfolk and the innovative solutions being developed.
- **Advocate for Change:** Contact your local Philippine consulate or embassy. Urge them to support initiatives like the Stealth Runner project that are working to protect our seas and empower our kababayans.
- **Connect Us with Resources:** Do you have connections to organizations or individuals who might be able to support the Stealth Runner project? Your network could be instrumental in securing the resources needed to expand our reach and impact.

Discover more from WPS News
Subscribe to get the latest posts sent to your email.

Dollars Don't Always Make Sense
Beyond the Bank Account: The True Measure of Wealth

In a world that often seems fixated on wealth and financial success, it's easy to fall into the trap of believing that the value of our lives is solely determined by the balance in our bank accounts. The notion that money is the ultimate metric for success and happiness is pervasive, but it is a limited and misguided perspective that fails to acknowledge the true richness of the human experience.

While financial security is undeniably important for meeting our basic needs and pursuing our aspirations, true wealth extends far beyond the confines of a bank statement. Here are some key points to consider when reflecting on the fallacy that everything in life is gauged solely by the amount of money in your bank account:

1. **Health and Well-being:** No amount of money can buy good health or genuine happiness. True wealth encompasses physical, mental, and emotional well-being, which are invaluable assets that cannot be quantified in monetary terms. Investing in self-care, meaningful relationships, and personal growth are essential components of a truly fulfilling life.

2. **Purpose and Fulfillment:** A sense of purpose and fulfillment derived from our passions, values, and contributions to society far outweighs the temporary satisfaction of material possessions. Engaging in meaningful work, pursuing our interests, and making a positive impact on the world around us are sources of wealth that transcend financial boundaries.

3. **Relationships and Connections:** The quality of our relationships and connections with others is a fundamental aspect of our overall well-being. Genuine friendships, loving family bonds, and a supportive community provide immeasurable wealth in the form of emotional support, companionship, and shared experiences that money cannot buy.

4. **Personal Growth and Learning:** Continuous personal growth, learning, and self-improvement are essential for leading a rich and fulfilling life. Engaging in new experiences, expanding our knowledge and skills, and challenging ourselves to grow beyond our comfort zones are invaluable sources of wealth that contribute to our overall development and satisfaction.

5. **Experiences and Memories:** The richness of life lies in the experiences we accumulate and the memories we create along the way. Traveling to new places, exploring different cultures, savoring moments of joy and laughter with loved ones—these are the treasures that enrich our lives and create lasting value far beyond the confines of material possessions.

In conclusion, while money certainly plays a role in providing us with opportunities and resources, it is essential to recognize that true wealth encompasses a much broader spectrum of values and experiences. By expanding our definition of wealth to include aspects such as health, purpose, relationships, personal growth, and experiences, we can cultivate a more holistic and fulfilling life that transcends the limitations of financial metrics. Ultimately, the true measure of wealth lies not in the amount of money in our bank accounts, but in the depth of our connections, the richness of our experiences, and the legacy of meaning and impact we leave behind.

Discover more from WPS News
Subscribe to get the latest posts sent to your email.

Globalization and Economic Power: China's Uncertain Future

In the '00s, many observers (professional and amateur) wrung their hands over the threat of an economically rising China. Quite a few people proclaimed that China owned the U.S.A. Asian Influence was written to explore the issue of China as an economic superpower.

It begins with a discussion about Japan in the 1990. There too is a warning that was not headed before 2007.

When the U.S. economy slid into the Peace Dividend[1] recession in the late 1980s and early 1990s, following the fall of the Soviet Union, Japan's economy faltered. The Japanese asset price bubble burst in 1990.

It cannot be overstated that Wealth, Women and War pointed to the obviously teetering house of cards in the USA.

You can purchase a copy of Wealth, Women, and War, but I would not suggest that you do that unless you need a hard copy for some reason. WordTechs Press released it back to me in May 2014, and I am making it available in blog form. Occupy asked that knowledge be shared, and in solidarity with Occupy Wall Street that is what I am doing. The only thing I can ask of you now is that you pay attention; we are not out of the woods yet.

Cliff Potts

September 25, 2014

Asian Influence

Japan, with a booming economy, and granted a Most Favored Nation status with the U.S., attempted to establish production facilities in the United States in the 1980s. However, Japanese culture was unfamiliar with the individualism of the U.S. citizens of the 1970s and 1980s. While any criticism of the Japanese or Japanese management style was met with cries of "White Racism" in the various trade journals, Japan's own critique of the U.S. as being a "Mongrel Nation" slipped quietly from the front pages. This was due in large part to the efforts of Robert Angel, a paid lobbyist for the Japanese government. He coined the term "Japan Bashing" to discredit critics of the Japanese imperialistic approach to trade.

While Japan enjoyed wide open markets in the United States, Japanese markets were closed to a free-flow of goods from the U.S. This remains a running argument in academic journals, as

Japan is cited as importing more goods per capita than the U.S. has imported from Japan. There may be some validity to this observation as Japan's population is approximately half that of the U.S. today.

When the U.S. economy slid into the Peace Dividend[1] recession in the late 1980s and early 1990s, following the fall of the Soviet Union, Japan's economy faltered. The Japanese asset price bubble burst in 1990.

This is another lesson concerning globalization. Any nation which produces goods specifically for consumption by another nation is liable to have its economy falter if the customer nation is no longer willing or able to consume the goods. Japan had done a poor job at developing its own consumer markets. While it did a phenomenal job of securing employment for its citizens, many of whom were still stunned by the abject poverty following World War Two, Japanese business could not be talked into spending the local economy back into prosperity. Even after the Japanese asset price bubble burst, Japanese citizens retained sufficient economic resources in liquid assets to recover from the economic slump. The same character traits, thrift and savings, which allowed them to recover after the war, stalled their economy during the 1990s. In today's globalized economy, there is much talk about China's rise to economic power. However, it is currently uncertain how well they are developing the internal market to consume their own goods and services. If China's economic boom is fully dependent on the U.S., or a Western, economy then an economic slow down in the West will devastate China as it did Japan in 1990. As sited in Morris Berman's Dark Ages America, China's approach to internal economic development is an expression of Social Darwinism – a current trend in the Free-Trade policies even in the US. This does not bode well for the internal picture of the Chinese economy. It cannot be overemphasized that The People's Republic of China is still a communist nation; effectively it is a national corporation where businesses are engaged in joint ventures with the government itself. While China may look good in the short term future, it is hard to predict what will occur over a longer period of time.

In A.M Sperber's *Murrow: His Life and Times*, it is cited that Edward R. Murrow, the voice of CBS during World War Two, worked hard as a young man to persuade colleges to hire Jewish scientists and other intellectual dissidents from Nazi Germany before the war broke out. Mr. Gates may be attempting to rescue the best intellectual assets of the world before regional chaos hits, by requesting more H-1B visas from Congress. Under the H-1B Visa program, recipients do not have to apply for political asylum and don't have to reveal the true nature of their move to U.S. protection. This also creates a pool of resources in the U.S. to pressure for change in the country of origin should that be needed. This, of course, is pure speculation, and as stated in the Wikipedia article on the H-1B visa, "Economist Milton Friedman has called the program a form of subsidy."[2] It does displace technical and engineering expertise in the U.S. and will remain a sore spot in U.S. labor relations in the foreseeable future.

China is nowhere near as stable as we have been led to believe. According to reports which have trickled through the broadcast of the BBC via NPR, recent Chinese defectors have warned the West of the risk of investing in China. The best summary is that China is unstable; however, the details are skeletal at best.

China seems to be heading toward some kind of economic crunch point not dissimilar to Japan's crisis in 1990. Two factors which are known are the threat of overheating the economy, and oddly enough, for a nation of 1.3 Billion people, a labor shortage.[3] China's population is growing old and a result of the zero population growth policies since 1979 (People's Republic of China's one-child policy), there is a shortage of young workers to fill slots at the entry levels of the economy.[4] There are serious issues concerning China's handling of Chinese dissidents, as well, according to a report co-authored by former Canadian cabinet minister David Kilgour and prominent rights lawyer David Matas released in July of 2006 stating that, "Chinese political prisoners, particularly Falun Gong[5] adherents, are being 'harvested' for the lucrative sale of organs to foreign buyers".[6]

There are unsubstantiated reports that the PRC (People's Republic of China) has transferred military equipment to provincial riot police to quell uprisings in various regions within China. The Chinese communist government may not be acting with astute wisdom in this period of economic boom. While all these charges and observations may seem somewhat sensationalized, there is an economic reality that cannot be overlooked: An economic boom is usually followed by a bust. There is no general indication how the current Chinese political culture will address the inevitable bust when one occurs.

India is equally threatened. Bangalore, the hub of India's technology and science based industries, is located on the Deccan Plateau in central India. It is vulnerable to aggression from a nuclear-armed Pakistan and a potentially unstable China. India has become one of the gathering points for western economic diversification. The net domestic product of Bangalore alone is estimated at 51.9 billion U.S. dollars.[7]

The economic viability of India may be its saving grace as far as China is concerned. China needs India as a gateway for further development. However, there is a highly volatile situation: Kashmir.

As was summarized in Radicals, Religion, and Revelation, "Kashmir is an 80,000 square mile region sandwiched between Pakistan and India. A Hindu monarch annexed this Islamic state into India. The fifty-year fight over this disputed claim has been marked by the exchange of artillery shells between the two nations. The world will likely see the first use of nuclear weapons since

World War II over this stretch of hilly land, each nation firing at the other's most strategic target."[8]

According to the article on Sino-Indian relations updated on April 30, 2007 in Wikipedia, "In November 2006, China and India had a verbal spat over claim of the north-east Indian state of Arunachal Pradesh. India claimed that China was occupying 38,000 square kilometers of its territory in Kashmir, while China claimed the whole of Arunachal Pradesh as its own.[9]

In a related article on Arunachal Pradesh, "The Chinese Ambassador to India, Sun Yuxi has publicly stated in India: "In our position, the whole of the state of Arunachal Pradesh is Chinese territory. And Tawang is only one of the places in it. We are claiming all of that. That is our position."[10] India's External Affairs Minister, Pranab Mukherjee, has countered that statement by saying that "Arunachal is an integral part of India."[11] India and China are currently engaged in talks to resolve the boundary question. Last year, both countries signed the "Political Parameters and Guiding Principles" document to peacefully resolve this issue."[12]

These events pit India against both China and Pakistan. The current President of Pakistan is Pervez Musharraf. He is a moderate Muslim in a nation which has a strong radical Islamic population. He has survived two separate assassination attempts. Both attempts bore the signature tactics of the Islamic radicals: suicide bombers. If, and it may be a big "if", the radical Islamic forces succeed in taking over Pakistan, they could inflict a serious blow to the economy of the United States by looking no further than central India. A conventional bombardment of Bangalore, let alone a nuclear strike, would seriously damage all western economies.

Under the ideal of globalization such threats are dismissed. History, however, shows what is good for business is not necessarily good for regional politics. In many respects, the destruction of World Trade Center towers in New York City did not do much to improve the prospects for peace through globalization. What the attack did achieve was to enhance the image of Al-Qaeda as a political force of liberation from Western Imperialism in Islamic lands, and created Osama bin Laden as a folk hero in Afghanistan, Iran, Palestine, Syria, Lebanon, Saudi Arabia, and Pakistan. Local politics are dismissed at the jeopardy of the corporation, even if the corporation's headquarters is thousands of miles away from the unstable region.

The business community declared that global war was not possible in the late 1800s and early 1900s because it would disrupt world trade. This was at the same time that Europe was engaged in an arms race. The same theme was being discussed before World War Two erupted. Once again, we hear this same argument. Today, it is called globalization. We hear that our business policies will prevail in bringing wayward nations into the global community. Commerce will pave the way to global harmony. This is being sung while Bill Gates tries to rescue the brain trust of India's and China's Information Technology fields, at the expense of the U.S. IT professionals, while the U.S. rattles the saber at Iran.

China Can Say No or The China That Can Say No: Political and Emotional Choices in the post Cold-War era (Pinyin: Zhongguo keyi shuo bu: Lengzhanhou shidai de zhengzhi yu qinggan jueze) is a 1996 Chinese non-fiction bestseller written and edited by Zhang Zangzang, Zhang Xiaobo, Song Qiang, Tang Zhengyu, Qiao Bian and Gu Qingsheng. It was published in China and strongly expresses Chinese nationalism. The book, which is modeled on The Japan That Can Say No, argues that many "fourth-generation" Chinese embraced Western values too strongly in the 1980s and disregarded their heritage and background. At least two of the authors participated in the Tiananmen Square protests of 1989. It specifically criticizes physicist Fang Lizhi and journalist Liu Binyan.

The book describes a disenchantment with the U.S. among the Chinese beginning in the 1990s, especially after the U.S. adopted a China containment strategy, rejected China's bid for the World Trade Organization, and worked against China's bid for the 2000 Summer Olympics. The authors criticize U.S. foreign policy and American individualism; they claim that China is used as a scapegoat for American problems.

The text also focuses on Japan, which is accused of being a client state of the U.S. and argues that Japan should not get a seat on the United Nations Security Council.[13]

---

[1] peace dividend, Definition: The reallocation of spending from military purposes to peacetime purposes, such as housing, education, and social projects. ("peace dividend." InvestorWords.Com. WebFinance, Inc, 2008. 7 Mar. 2008 http://www.investorwords.com/3644/peace_dividend.html).

[2] H-1B visa. (2008, June 17). In Wikipedia, The Free Encyclopedia. Retrieved 01:56, June 18, 2008, from http://en.wikipedia.org/w/index.php?title=H-1B_visa&oldid=219840555

[3] Economy of the People's Republic of China. (2007, April 29). In Wikipedia, The Free Encyclopedia. Retrieved 17:27, May 2, 2007, from http://en.wikipedia.org/w/index.php?title=Economy_of_the_People%27s_Republic_of_China&oldid=126921841

[4] Demography of the People's Republic of China. (2007, April 29). In Wikipedia, The Free Encyclopedia. Retrieved 17:27, May 2, 2007, from http://en.wikipedia.org/w/index.php?title=Demography_of_the_People%27s_Republic_of_China&oldid=126910697

[5] falun gong – a spiritual movement that began in China in the latter half of the 20th century and is based on Buddhist and Taoist teachings and practices ("falun gong." WordNet 3.0, Farlex clipart collection. 2003-2007. Princeton University, Clipart.com, Farlex Inc. 7 Mar. 2008 http://www.thefreedictionary.com/falun+gong)

[6] Human rights in the People's Republic of China. (2007, May 2). In Wikipedia, The Free Encyclopedia. Retrieved 17:22, May 2, 2007, from http://en.wikipedia.org/w/index.php?title=Human_rights_in_the_People%27s_Republic_of_China&oldid=127677276

[7] Economy of Bangalore. (2007, May 2). In Wikipedia, The Free Encyclopedia. Retrieved 17:46, May 2, 2007, from http://en.wikipedia.org/w/index.php?title=Economy_of_Bangalore&oldid=127587393

[8] Potts, Clifford A. Radicals, Religion, and Revelation. Dallas: WordTechs Press, 2008. p. 65

[9] Sino-Indian relations." (2007, April 30). In Wikipedia, The Free Encyclopedia. Retrieved 17:56, May 2, 2007, from http://en.wikipedia.org/w/index.php?title=Sino-Indian_relations&oldid=127013002

[10] Arunachal Pradesh is our territory: Chinese envoy. (2006, November 14). Rediff India Abroad . Retrieved June 17, 2008, from http://www.rediff.com/news/2006/nov/14china.htm

[11] Singh, O. (2006, November 28). Arunachal integral part of India: Pranab in Parliament. Rediff India Abroad . Retrieved June 17, 2008, from http://www.rediff.com/news/2006/nov/28jintao.htm

[12] Arunachal Pradesh. (2007, April 29). In Wikipedia, The Free Encyclopedia. Retrieved 18:04, May 2, 2007, from http://en.wikipedia.org/w/index.php?title=Arunachal_Pradesh&oldid=126924899

[13] China Can Say No. (2007, April 12). In Wikipedia, The Free Encyclopedia. Retrieved 19:28, May 1, 2007, from http://en.wikipedia.org/w/index.php?title=China_Can_Say_No&oldid=122202767

Join the Stealth Runner Project for a Sustainable Future

The Stealth Runner Project Needs You
Calling all Kababayans abroad!

The Philippines, our beautiful island nation, has always relied on the strength and resilience of its fisherfolk. Today, they face a growing threat in the West Philippine Sea – overfishing, illegal fishing practices, and dwindling resources. The Stealth Runner project is rising to meet this challenge, and we need your support.

More Than Just a Boat:

The Stealth Runner isn't just another patrol vessel. These innovative boats are built with locally sourced, sustainable materials, minimizing their environmental impact. Their quiet engines allow for stealthy patrols, promoting responsible fishing practices and protecting marine life.

Empowering Our People:

The Stealth Runner project goes beyond safeguarding the seas; it's about empowering Filipino fisherfolk. By providing them with the tools and support they need to operate safely and sustainably, the project ensures the future of this vital industry.

Your Connection Matters:

As a Filipino expat, you understand the importance of our maritime heritage and the challenges faced back home. Here's how you can make a difference:

- Spread Awareness: Share the story of the Stealth Runner project with your network. Let others know about this innovative solution that protects Filipino fisherfolk and the West Philippine Sea.
- Become a Donor: Your contribution, no matter how big or small, can help build and maintain the Stealth Runner fleet. Every peso helps secure a brighter future for our kababayans.
- Volunteer Your Expertise: Do you have skills in fundraising, communications, or maritime operations? The Stealth Runner project welcomes your expertise. Help us navigate the challenges and achieve our goals.

Together, we can ensure a future where Filipino fisherfolk continue to thrive, safeguarding our precious seas for generations to come.

- Spread the Word: Share our story on social media, tell your friends and family, and help us raise awareness about the Stealth Runner project.
- Volunteer Your Skills: We're always looking for talented individuals to join our team. Whether you have marketing expertise, nautical experience, or simply a passion for helping others, we welcome your contribution.

Together, we can empower Filipino fisherfolk, protect the marine environment, and ensure a sustainable future for the West Philippine Sea. Let's make a wave of change!

Discover more from WPS News
Subscribe to get the latest posts sent to your email.

Heightened Tensions in the West Philippine Sea: A Cause for Concern

Update| 24 September 2024 7:48 PM

The West Philippine Sea, a contested region in the South China Sea, has been a flashpoint for tensions between the Philippines and China for years. Recent developments suggest that these tensions may be reaching a boiling point.

Record Number of Chinese Vessels

According to a report by ABS-CBN News, the number of Chinese vessels in the West Philippine Sea has reached a record high of 251 1. This comes after the departure of a Philippine Coast Guard vessel from the area. The increase in Chinese presence is seen by many as a provocative move by China to assert its territorial claims in the region.

Philippine Response

The Philippine government has responded to China's actions by deploying warships and a coast guard ship to monitor Chinese activities in the West Philippine Sea 3. The Philippines has also acquired new Israeli-made missile boats to bolster its navy's capabilities 2.

Lack of Transparency

However, there are concerns that the Philippine government is not being transparent about its plans for dealing with China in the West Philippine Sea 4. Some critics argue that the government is not doing enough to defend Philippine territory.

OSINT Analysis

Open-source intelligence (OSINT) can provide valuable insights into the situation in the West Philippine Sea. For example, satellite imagery can be used to track the movements of Chinese vessels in the region. Social media can also be used to monitor public opinion on the issue. By analyzing OSINT, the Philippine government can gain a better understanding of China's intentions and develop more effective strategies for responding to them.

Looking Ahead

The situation in the West Philippine Sea is complex and constantly evolving. It is clear that tensions between the Philippines and China are on the rise. The Philippine government needs to develop a clear and comprehensive strategy for dealing with China in order to protect its national interests.

Additional Notes

This blog post is based on information from the following sources:
- ABS-CBN News
- Philippine News Agency
- Inquirer.net
- Rappler
- Inquirer.net

It is important to note that these sources may have biases. It is always a good idea to consult a variety of sources to get a well-rounded view of the issue.

Discover more from WPS News

Subscribe to get the latest posts sent to your email.

Beyond Celebrity: Why Real Change Starts with Everyday People

We live in a world obsessed with celebrity. From actors and musicians to politicians and tech gurus, our attention is constantly drawn to charismatic figures promising solutions to complex problems. But what if the answer to the world's issues doesn't lie in idolizing celebrities, but in the collective power of everyday people?

The Allure of the Celebrity Savior

There's a seductive comfort in the idea of a single, heroic figure swooping in to fix everything. We see it reflected in superhero movies and political campaigns that paint candidates as infallible leaders. But this celebrity worship can be a dangerous distraction. It breeds a culture of passivity, where we expect others to solve our problems for us.

The Issues with Celebrity Solutions

- Celebrity Disconnect: Celebrities, by nature, are often far removed from the daily struggles of ordinary people. Their solutions might not address the real needs on the ground.
- The Cult of Personality: Focusing on personalities overshadows the actual policies and ideas. We get caught up in charisma rather than critically evaluating solutions.
- Short-Term Fixes: Celebrity solutions often prioritize grabbing headlines over lasting change. They might address symptoms but fail to tackle root causes.

The Power of Everyday People

Real change, on the other hand, is a slow and steady process driven by the collective action of ordinary people. Here's why everyday people hold the key to a better future:

Closer to the Issues: Everyday people experience problems firsthand. They have a deep understanding of the challenges in their communities.

Long-Term Commitment: They are more likely to be invested in lasting solutions that will affect their own lives and the lives of future generations.

Collective Power: When ordinary people come together, their collective voice can be a powerful force for change.

Moving Beyond Celebrity Worship

This doesn't mean we should completely ignore celebrities. They can be valuable allies in raising awareness about important issues. But true change requires a shift in focus. Here's what we can do:

Support Grassroots Movements: Look for organizations working on solutions in your community. Donate your time, skills, or resources.
Hold Leaders Accountable: Don't blindly follow politicians or celebrities. Scrutinize their policies and hold them accountable for their actions.
Empower Yourself: Educate yourself about the issues that matter to you. Get involved in local politics. Be the change you want to see.
Conclusion

The world's problems are complex and there are no easy fixes. But by moving beyond celebrity worship and embracing the power of everyday people, we can build a more just and sustainable future. Remember, the most important changemakers aren't on a red carpet, they're in our communities, working tirelessly to make a difference. Let's join them.

Discover more from WPS News
Subscribe to get the latest posts sent to your email.

Typhon Missile System: A Game Changer for Philippine Defense

The US-Made Typhon Missile System: Boosting Philippine Defense or Stirring Trouble?

The Philippines, strategically located in the South China Sea, has recently expressed interest in acquiring the Medium Range Capability (MRC) Typhon Missile System from the United States. This potential deal has sparked discussions about its impact on Philippine defense capabilities, regional security dynamics, and legal considerations under existing international agreements.

What is the Typhon Missile System?

Developed by Raytheon Missiles & Defense, the Typhon is a land-based, surface-to-surface missile system designed for medium-range precision strikes. Here's a breakdown of its technical specifications:

- Range: Up to 300 kilometers (186 miles) depending on the missile variant.
- Payload: Carries various warheads, including high-explosive and anti-ship missiles.
- Mobility: Highly mobile launchers mounted on wheeled vehicles for rapid deployment.
- Guidance: Utilizes GPS and inertial navigation for precise targeting.

Boosting Philippine Defense

Proponents of the Typhon system argue that it would significantly enhance Philippine defense capabilities. Here are some key points:

- Deterrence: The extended range and firepower of the Typhon could deter potential aggressors in the region.
- Island Defense: The system's mobility allows for deployment on various islands, strengthening Philippine territorial defense.
- Precision Strikes: The Typhon's precision targeting minimizes collateral damage compared to traditional artillery.
- Legal Ramifications and Regional Tensions

However, the acquisition of the Typhon system also raises several legal and geopolitical concerns:

- MTCR Compliance: The Philippines is a signatory to the Missile Technology Control Regime (MTCR), which restricts the proliferation of certain missile technologies. The Typhon's range might raise concerns about compliance.
- China Factor: China views the South China Sea as its territorial water and might see the deployment of the Typhon system as a threat, potentially escalating regional tensions.
- Arms Race: The introduction of advanced weaponry could trigger an arms race in Southeast Asia, destabilizing the region.

The Road Ahead

The decision to acquire the Typhon system requires careful consideration by the Philippine government. It's crucial to weigh the potential benefits for national defense against the legal and geopolitical risks. Open discussions and transparency with regional neighbors are essential for maintaining peace and stability.

WPS.News will continue to monitor this developing story and provide updates on the potential acquisition of the Typhon Missile System by the Philippines.

Discover more from WPS News
Subscribe to get the latest posts sent to your email.

Revolutionizing Maritime Tech: The Stealth Runner Explained

Unveiling the Tech Behind the Stealth Runner

Tech Meets Tradition: The Stealth Runner Project's Locally Sourced, Tech-Powered Patrol Boat

The *Stealth Runner project* isn't just about safeguarding Filipino fisherfolk; it's about pioneering a new era in sustainable maritime technology. This innovative patrol boat is a fusion of tradition and cutting-edge solutions, designed to meet the unique challenges of the West Philippine Sea.

Locally Sourced Strength:

The Stealth Runner's robust hull is built with locally sourced, sustainable wood. This not only minimizes the project's environmental footprint, but also pays homage to the traditional boatbuilding skills honed by Filipino artisans for generations.

Silent Power:

Unlike noisy trawlers that disrupt marine life, the *Stealth Runner* employs a specially designed, near-silent engine. This allows the crew to approach fish without spooking them, promoting selective fishing and minimizing bycatch.

Tech for Transparency:

The Stealth Runner is equipped with advanced GPS and communication systems. This real-time data collection allows for better patrol coordination and improved monitoring of illegal fishing activities in the West Philippine Sea.

A Pioneering Solution:

The Stealth Runner project stands as a beacon of innovation in sustainable maritime technology. Its unique blend of local materials, eco-friendly features, and advanced technology paves the way for a future where patrol and support vessels operate with minimal environmental impact.

Calling All Maritime Enthusiasts!

Are you a passionate sailor or a tech-savvy maritime expert? The Stealth Runner project welcomes your expertise! Volunteer your knowledge to help maintain and operate these innovative vessels.

Spread the Word!

Share the story of the *Stealth Runner* project with fellow maritime enthusiasts. By generating awareness, we can create a powerful wave of support for this pioneering approach to sustainable ocean protection.

Help Us Build a Brighter Future for the West Philippine Sea!

The Stealth Runner project relies on the support of passionate individuals like you. Your contributions, big or small, can make a real difference. Here's how you can get involved:

- Donate: Every dollar helps us build and equip these essential vessels. Visit our donation page at patreon.com/AllenGuadalupe
- Spread the Word: Share our story on social media, tell your friends and family, and help us raise awareness about the Stealth Runner project.
- Volunteer Your Skills: We're always looking for talented individuals to join our team. Whether you have marketing expertise, nautical experience, or simply a passion for helping others, we welcome your contribution.
- Join the Crew: Are you a skilled mariner who wants to make a positive impact? We're building a team to operate the Stealth Runner fleet.

Together, we can empower Filipino fisherfolk, protect the marine environment, and ensure a sustainable future for the West Philippine Sea. Let's make a wave of change!

Discover more from WPS News
Subscribe to get the latest posts sent to your email.

Stock Your 72-Hour Kit: Must-Have Vitamins

Essential Vitamins for Your 72-Hour Emergency Kit: A Guide for Baybay City Residents

In the face of an emergency, having a well-stocked 72-hour survival kit is crucial. While food, water, and first-aid supplies are top priorities, including essential vitamins shouldn't be overlooked. These micronutrients play a vital role in maintaining your health and resilience during a crisis.

Here's a breakdown of some key vitamins to consider for your 72-hour kit, specifically tailored for residents of Baybay City:

Vitamin D: Baybay City enjoys abundant sunshine, but during emergencies, sun exposure might be limited. Vitamin D helps regulate calcium absorption, crucial for bone health and muscle function. Consider including 1,000 IU of Vitamin D3 in your kit.

Vitamin C: This antioxidant supports your immune system, vital for fighting off infections during stressful situations. Include 500mg of Vitamin C daily.

B-Complex Vitamins: These vitamins play a vital role in energy production and maintaining a healthy nervous system. A B-Complex supplement containing Vitamins B1, B2, B3, B5, B6, B12, and Folic Acid is recommended.

Vitamin E: Another antioxidant, Vitamin E protects cells from damage and supports immune function. Include 400 IU of Vitamin E daily.
General Considerations:

Storage: Choose chewable or liquid multivitamins for ease of consumption without water. Ensure airtight containers and prioritize vitamins with extended expiry dates.

Personal Needs: If you have pre-existing medical conditions, consult your doctor for specific vitamin recommendations that complement your existing medications.

Dietary Restrictions: For those with dietary restrictions, consider vegan or vegetarian formulations of essential vitamins.
Optimizing Your 72-Hour Kit:

A well-prepared 72-hour kit should be lightweight and portable, allowing for easy movement in case of evacuation. Rotate your vitamin stock regularly to ensure they remain within expiry dates. Remember, a well-stocked 72-hour kit provides peace of mind and promotes overall well-being during emergencies.

Remember: This information is intended for general knowledge only and shouldn't be a substitute for professional medical advice. Always consult your doctor for personalized recommendations.

Discover more from WPS News
Subscribe to get the latest posts sent to your email.

Geopolitical Insights: Why I Write for Free

Why I Write for Free: Independent Geopolitical Insights for a Complex World

Here at WPS.News, you won't find hidden agendas or sensationalized reporting. I write for free, with no advertisements or sponsorships, because my mission is to empower the global community with the information they need to navigate the complexities of geopolitics.

This isn't about self-promotion. It's about equipping you with the knowledge to make informed decisions in the face of a rapidly changing world.

Why Short, Focused Essays?

My approach is to deliver concise, daily articles that provide actionable insights for the day or week ahead. I also offer broader analyses that inform your long-term planning for the next five years. This aligns perfectly with the WPS.News model of fostering strategic foresight.

Committed to Accuracy and Transparency

As of today, September 23rd, 2024 (marking the 13th anniversary of Occupy Chicago's inception), I'm offering a detailed breakdown of the *Stealth Runner* Project schedule through March 2025. My commitment is to keep you informed with reliable, factual information, avoiding sensationalism and conspiracy theories.

Key Events in the Indo-Pacific Region (August 23rd to September 22nd, 2024)

Geopolitical Tensions

- China-Taiwan Relations: Tensions between China and Taiwan remained high. China continued its military exercises near Taiwan, asserting its sovereignty over the island.
- South China Sea Disputes: The ongoing territorial disputes in the South China Sea, involving China, Vietnam, the Philippines, Brunei, Malaysia, and Indonesia, persisted. There were reports of increased naval activity and maritime incidents in the region.
- India-China Border Standoff: The long-standing border standoff between India and China in the Himalayas continued, with both sides maintaining a strong military presence.
- Economic Developments

- Regional Trade Agreements: Several countries in the Indo-Pacific region continued to negotiate and implement regional trade agreements, such as the Regional Comprehensive Economic Partnership (RCEP) and the Comprehensive and Progressive Agreement for Trans-Pacific Partnership (CPTPP).
- Infrastructure Projects: China's Belt and Road Initiative (BRI) continued to gain momentum in the region, with various infrastructure projects underway in countries like Indonesia, the Philippines, and Malaysia.
- Climate Change and Environmental Issues
- Extreme Weather Events: The region experienced several extreme weather events, including typhoons, floods, and heatwaves, highlighting the impacts of climate change.
- Conservation Efforts: There were ongoing efforts to protect biodiversity and address environmental challenges, such as deforestation and pollution.

Other Notable Events

ASEAN Summit: The Association of Southeast Asian Nations (ASEAN) held its annual summit, focusing on regional cooperation, economic integration, and security issues.
Military Exercises: Several countries in the region conducted joint military exercises and defense cooperation initiatives.
Stay Informed, Stay Empowered

By subscribing to and sharing my work, you'll gain valuable insights into the evolving geopolitical landscape. My goal is to equip you with the knowledge you need to navigate the coming chapters of our shared history.

Discover more from WPS News
Subscribe to get the latest posts sent to your email.

Understanding the Scarborough Shoal Dispute: Key Events and Implications

The Scarborough Shoal Standoff: A History of Tension in the South China Sea (Last

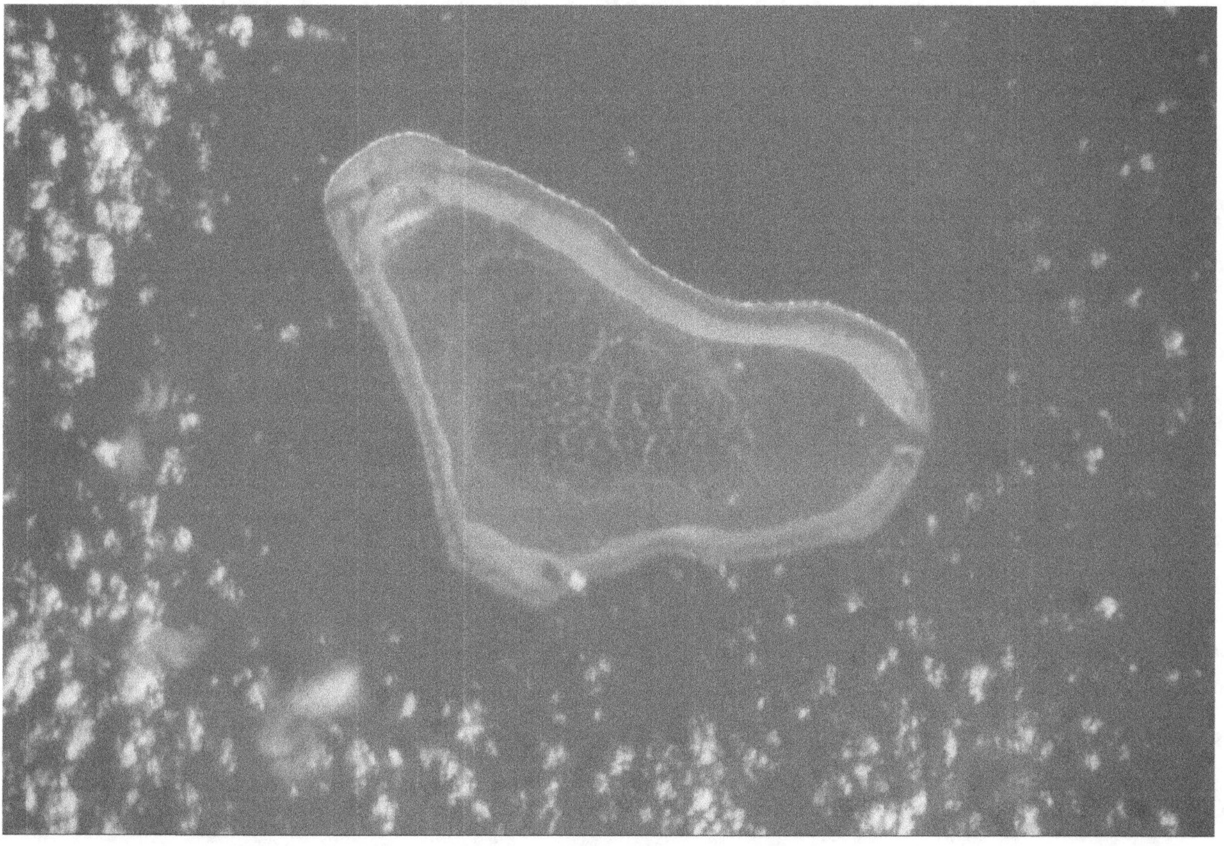

Updated: September 28, 2024)

The Scarborough Shoal, a tiny boomerang-shaped outcrop in the South China Sea, has been a flashpoint for tension between China and the Philippines for over a decade. Here's a timeline of key events that have unfolded since the first incident:

2012: A standoff erupts after Philippine authorities arrest Chinese fishermen operating near the shoal. The Philippines, citing its sovereign rights within its Exclusive Economic Zone (EEZ), impounds the fishing vessel. China retaliates by deploying maritime surveillance vessels, escalating tensions. The Philippines eventually releases the fishermen, but tensions remain high.

2013: The Philippines initiates arbitration proceedings against China's expansive claims in the South China Sea under the United Nations Convention on the Law of the Sea (UNCLOS).

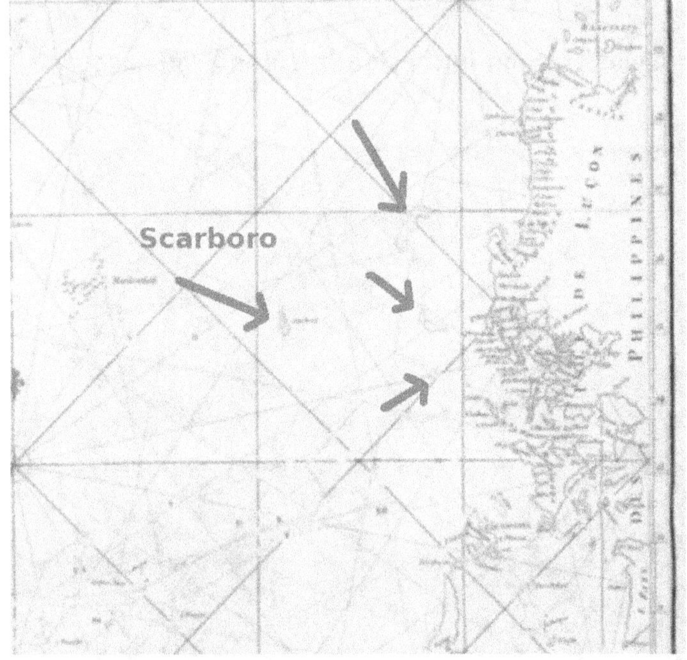

2016: The Permanent Court of Arbitration in The Hague issues a landmark ruling, declaring China's claims to historic rights over most of the South China Sea to be without legal basis. The ruling also affirms the Philippines' sovereign rights within its EEZ, including the Scarborough Shoal. China rejects the ruling.

2017: Following the Hague ruling, there's a period of relative calm. However, Chinese coast guard and fishing vessels continue to maintain a presence near the shoal, occasionally harassing Filipino fishermen.

2019: A new incident flares up when a Philippine patrol vessel confronts a Chinese survey ship operating within the Philippines' EEZ near the Scarborough Shoal. The standoff continues for several weeks before the Chinese vessel eventually withdraws.

2020: Throughout 2020, reports emerge of an increased Chinese presence near the shoal, with concerns growing about China's intentions. There are also reports of Chinese militia vessels harassing Filipino fishermen and intimidating Philippine coast guard forces.

Present (September 2024): The situation remains tense, with continued reports of Chinese activity near the Scarborough Shoal. The Philippines has expressed concern about China's growing assertiveness and its disregard for international law.

Analysis of War Risk:

While the Scarborough Shoal situation is undeniably concerning, it's difficult to definitively assess the immediate threat of war. Here's a look at some factors to consider:

- **China's Growing Military:** China has been rapidly modernizing its military, particularly its naval capabilities. This has led to concerns about China's potential to use force to assert its claims in the South China Sea.

- **Escalating Tensions:** The increasing frequency and intensity of incidents like those at Scarborough Shoal raise the risk of miscalculation or unintended escalation.
- **US Involvement:** The United States has a long-standing commitment to freedom of navigation in the South China Sea and has repeatedly challenged China's expansive claims. The US maintains a strong military presence in the region, which could serve as a deterrent to Chinese aggression.
- **Diplomatic Efforts:** Despite the tensions, both China and the Philippines have engaged in diplomatic efforts to manage the situation. Both countries are aware of the devastating consequences of a full-blown military conflict.

Conclusion:

The situation at the Scarborough Shoal is a stark reminder of the ongoing tensions in the South China Sea. While the immediate threat of war may be difficult to gauge, China's increasing assertiveness and disregard for international law remain a cause for concern. Continued diplomatic efforts, coupled with a firm commitment to upholding international law, are crucial to avoid a wider conflict in the Indo-Pacific.

The tension sparked by China's encroachment on Philippine territory began twelve years ago. Children have grown up since China unilaterally decided to steal resources from its less populated neighbors. China's "Gray Zone" tactics have thus far been effective. The world largely ignored China's encroachments until very recently. Since 2023, everyone in the region has been increasing their military expenditures due to China's actions. While many have suggested that this situation resembles a path to war, that may not necessarily be the case. Xi Jinping could pass away, and a new CCP leader might prioritize China's internal issues. As John Connor famously said, "The future's not set. There's no fate but what we make for ourselves."

Sources:

The Permanent Court of Arbitration: The South China Sea Arbitration (2016)
Council on Foreign Relations: China's Maritime Dispute with the Philippines
The Diplomat: Why the Scarborough Shoal Dispute Matters

Discover more from WPS News
Subscribe to get the latest posts sent to your email.

Challenging the Emperor's Illusions: Embracing Critical Thinking

Yup, He is Naked!

In reflecting on my journey, it has become clear to me that the path to wealth and comfort, the freedom to pursue my passions without fear of judgment or persecution, has been a challenging one. I have often felt overlooked and undervalued for my ability to think critically, to offer insights that may challenge the prevailing norms of our society.

It is disheartening to see how those who dare to question, to think beyond the confines of accepted wisdom, are sometimes met with indifference or resistance. The richness of diverse perspectives and the power of critical thinking should be embraced, not stifled. I believe that society would benefit greatly from recognizing and honoring the contributions of individuals who offer unique insights and perspectives.

As I sit here contemplating on this Sunday afternoon, I am reminded of the importance of fostering a culture that values intellectual diversity and encourages thoughtful dialogue. The naked truth of the emperor's illusions serves as a reminder that we must be open to perspectives that may challenge our beliefs and push us towards growth and progress.

I hope that as a society, we can move towards a more inclusive and open-minded approach, where the voices of critical thinkers are not just heard but respected. It is through this mutual respect and appreciation for different viewpoints that we can truly thrive and evolve as a community.

The Philippines' Quest for a Robust Missile Defense System: A Strategic Necessity

The Philippines, an archipelago nation strategically located in the South China Sea, faces a complex security landscape. Territorial disputes, maritime security challenges, and the ever-evolving nature of warfare necessitate a robust and modernized defense system. In this context, the recent call by the Armed Forces of the Philippines (AFP) Chief of Staff, General Romeo Brawner Jr., for the acquisition of the US-made Typhon Missile System signifies a critical step towards bolstering the country's missile defense capabilities.

The impetus for a comprehensive missile defense system stems from the ongoing modernization program of the AFP. This program, guided by the Comprehensive Archipelagic Defense Concept (CADC), aims to transform the AFP into a more credible and capable force. The CADC recognizes the archipelagic nature of the Philippines and emphasizes the need for a multi-layered defense strategy encompassing air, maritime, and land domains. A critical component of this strategy is the development of a potent missile defense system.

General Brawner's request for the Typhon Missile System highlights the specific capabilities the AFP seeks to acquire. The Typhon system is a land-based surface-to-surface missile system known for its versatility. It can launch various missiles, including the Tomahawk Land Attack Missile and the Standard Missile-6. The Tomahawk Land Attack Missile offers long-range precision strike capabilities, while the Standard Missile-6 provides robust anti-air defense against aerial threats.

The integration of such a system into the Philippine defense apparatus would significantly enhance the country's ability to address contemporary security challenges. The long-range strike capabilities of the Tomahawk Land Attack Missile would enable the AFP to deter and counter potential aggressors. This deterrence could prove particularly valuable in the context of the ongoing territorial disputes in the South China Sea. Additionally, the Standard Missile-6's anti-air defense capabilities would strengthen the Philippines' capacity to safeguard its airspace from missile attacks and hostile aircraft.

The envisioned "integrated defense" outlined in the CADC goes beyond the mere acquisition of weapon systems. It emphasizes the importance of developing a network of sensors, radars, and communication systems that can effectively detect, track, and engage incoming threats. The Typhon Missile System, when integrated with such a network, would form a crucial node in this integrated defense architecture.

However, the pursuit of a robust missile defense system is not without its challenges. The high cost of acquiring and maintaining such advanced weaponry is a significant consideration. The Philippines must carefully weigh the economic implications of such an endeavor while ensuring the long-term sustainability of its defense modernization program.

Furthermore, the geopolitical complexities of the region must be navigated with prudence. The introduction of advanced missile systems could potentially trigger concerns among neighboring countries. The Philippines must strive for transparency in its defense modernization efforts and engage in confidence-building measures to alleviate any apprehensions.

In conclusion, the Philippines' quest for a comprehensive missile defense system, as exemplified by the request for the Typhon Missile System, is a strategic imperative. It aligns with the goals of the AFP modernization program and the CADC, bolstering the country's deterrence capabilities and safeguarding its territorial integrity. While challenges exist in terms of cost and regional considerations, a well-planned and transparent approach can ensure the successful development of a robust missile defense system, ultimately contributing to a more secure and stable Philippines.

Source: PH needs comprehensive missile defense system: AFP chief

Discover more from WPS News
Subscribe to get the latest posts sent to your email.

American Man Convicted of Mercenary Charges in Russia Raises Questions (WPS.News)

Baybay City, Philippines – September 30, 2024

A recent case involving a 72-year-old American man, Alexander Drueke, convicted of mercenary charges in Russia, has sparked debate about the nature of foreign fighters in the ongoing Ukraine conflict. Drueke, alongside two other captured fighters, was sentenced to death by a Donetsk court in June 2024.

The article linked here, from Radio Free Europe / Radio Liberty (RFE/RL), details the case and the controversy surrounding it. Let's delve deeper into the key aspects of this story.

The Question of Mercenaries

The label "mercenary" carries a specific legal definition. Mercenaries are typically defined as foreign fighters motivated primarily by financial gain rather than ideological or nationalistic reasons. They are not considered lawful combatants under international humanitarian law and can be prosecuted if captured.

The Ukrainian government maintains that Drueke and the other captured fighters were volunteers who joined the Ukrainian military to defend the country. However, Russia argues that they were mercenaries due to their lack of prior military experience and alleged recruitment through private military companies.

Can a 72-Year-Old be a Mercenary?

The age of the accused raises questions about the mercenary label. While there's no upper age limit for mercenary activities, the physical demands of combat are typically associated with younger fighters. Drueke's case suggests a potential complication in the definition of mercenaries, particularly when considering motivations beyond physical combat capabilities.

While a full picture of Drueke's motivations remains unclear, here are some points to consider when evaluating the mercenary charges:

Volunteer Motive: Drueke's decision to fight alongside Ukrainians could be driven by ideological support for Ukraine's cause, not financial gain.

Military Experience: While Drueke reportedly lacked recent military experience, prior service or combat training doesn't necessarily define mercenary status.

Foreign Fighters vs. Mercenaries: The distinction between foreign fighters and mercenaries is often blurred. International law allows for foreign volunteers to join national militaries during conflicts.

Conclusion

The Drueke case highlights the complexities surrounding foreign fighters in the Ukraine conflict. Further investigation is needed to understand Drueke's motivations definitively. However, his age and the possibility of ideological reasons for joining the fight raise doubts about the validity of the mercenary charges.

Stay informed with WPS.News for further developments on this story.

Source: American, 72, Reportedly Pleads Guilty To Mercenary Charge In Moscow

Corrections:
Alexander (Alex) Drueke is 40, not 72 as initially reported.

Two US military veterans, Alex Drueke and Andy Tai Ngoc Huynh, who were captured by Russian forces while volunteering to fight in Ukraine, have been released and returned to the United States. The release was part of a prisoner swap mediated by Saudi Arabia. The two men, who were held for several months,

endured harsh conditions and were forced to make statements under duress. Upon their return, they expressed gratitude for the support they received and emphasized the importance of continued support for Ukraine in its fight against Russian aggression.

Discover more from WPS News
Subscribe to get the latest posts sent to your email.